W9-AYC-387

WILD TURKEY HUNTING

©1991 by National Rifle Association of America
Third Edition

Library of Congress Catalog Card Number;
90-083405

Main entry under title:
Wild Turkey Hunting—NRA Hunter Skills Series

ISBN 0-935998-74-8

08680 (paperback)   3/99

ACKNOWLEDGEMENTS

Authors

Mike Strandlund, Outdoor Writer and former Staffer, NRA Hunter Services
Earl Hower, Former Staffer, NRA Hunter Services

Editors

Mike Strandlund, Outdoor Writer and former Staffer, NRA Hunter Services
Robert L. Davis Jr., Manager, NRA Hunter Services

Production Manager

Earl Hower, Former Staffer, NRA Hunter Services

Illustrator

Doug Pifer, Former Staffer, NRA Hunter Services

Co-Authors and Review Committee

Rob Keck, Former Member, NRA Hunting and Wildlife Conservation Committee and Executive Vice President, National Wild Turkey Federation
Jim Norine, Former Director, NRA Hunter Services Division
Dennis Eggers, Regional Director, NRA Field Operations Division
Robert L. Davis, Jr., Manager, Hunter Services
Montgomery S. Embrey, Program Coordinator, NRA Hunter Services
Barry Winner, Former Staffer, NRA Hunter Services
Doug Pifer, Former Staffer, NRA Hunter Services
Karl J. Gunzer, Jr., Former Staffer, NRA Hunter Services
Carl Brown, Director of Chapter and Membership Development, National Wild Turkey Federation
Jim Clay, President, Perfection Turkey Calls, Inc.
Dick Kirby, President, Quaker Boy Game Calls, Inc. and Member National Wild Turkey Federation Board of Directors
John Metzger, Professional Turkey Guide

James E. Miller, U.S. Department of Agriculture—Extension Service and Member, National Wild Turkey Federation Technical Committee

Dave Streb, General Manager, Quaker Boy Game Calls and former Member, National Wild Turkey Federation Board of Directors

Robby Rohm, Call Maker, Rohm Brothers Turkey Calls

Tom Stuckey, Champion Turkey Caller

E. Sam Nenno, Wildlife Biologist, formerly with U.S. Forest Service and Penn's Woods Products, Inc.

R. Wayne Bailey, Wildlife Biologist-Retired, North Carolina Wildlife Resource Commission and West Virginia Department of Natural Resources

The National Rifle Association is grateful for the contributions made by the preceding persons, by the National Wild Turkey Federation, and by the government agencies credited throughout this book.

Photo Credits

Front and Back Cover Photos By **Mike Strandlund**

NRA Hunter's Code of Ethics

I will consider myself an invited guest of the landowner, seeking his permission, and conduct myself so that I may be welcome in the future.

I will obey the rules of safe gun handling and will courteously but firmly insist that others who hunt with me do the same.

I will obey all game laws and regulations, and will insist that my companions do likewise.

I will do my best to acquire marksmanship and hunting skills that assure clean, sportsmanlike kills.

I will support conservation efforts that assure good hunting for future generations of Americans.

I will pass along to younger hunters the attitudes and skills essential to a true outdoor sportsman.

NRA Gun Safety Rules

The fundamental NRA rules for safe gun handling are:

- Always keep the gun pointed in a safe direction.
- Always keep your finger off the trigger until ready to shoot.
- Always keep the gun unloaded until ready to use.

When using or storing a gun always follow these NRA rules:

- Be sure the gun is safe to operate.
- Know how to safely use the gun.
- Use only the correct ammunition for your gun.
- Know your target and what is beyond.
- Wear eye and ear protection as appropriate.
- Never use alcohol or drugs before or while shooting.
- Store guns so they are not accessible to unauthorized persons.

Be aware that certain types of guns and many shooting activities require additional safety precautions.

To learn more about gun safety, enroll in an NRA hunter clinic or state hunter education class, or an NRA safety training or basic marksmanship course.

TODAY'S AMERICAN HUNTER

If you're a hunter, you're one of 17 million Americans who love the outdoors, have a close tie with traditions, and help conserve our natural resources. You know the thrill and beauty of a duck blind at dawn, a whitetail buck sneaking past your stand, a hot-headed, bugling bull elk. With your friends and forefathers you share the rich traditions of knowing wild places and good hunting dogs. Your woodsmanship and appreciation of nature provide food for body and soul.

And through contributions to hunting licenses and stamps, conservation tax funds, and sportsman clubs, you are partly responsible for the dramatic recovery of wildlife and its habitat. Hunters can take great pride—and satisfaction that only hunters know—in the great increases of deer, turkeys, elk, some waterfowl, and other species over the last century.

Your involvement with the National Rifle Association of America is also important to promote conservation and sportsmanship. In NRA, concerned hunters and shooters work together for laws and programs of benefit to the shooting sports. Most important is the education of sportsmen through programs like the nationwide Hunter Clinic Program operated by the NRA Hunter Services Department. Through the program and the Hunter Skills Series of how-to-hunting books, America's already admirable hunters can keep improving their skills, safety, responsibility, and sportsmanship to help ensure our country's rich hunting traditions flourish forever.

CONTENTS

Page

Introduction ix

Part I: Before the Hunt 1

Chapter 1—Biology and Behavior of the Wild Turkey 3

Chapter 2—Turkey Calls and Calling 27

Chapter 3—Guns, Bows, and Turkeys 45

Chapter 4—Gearing Up for Gobblers 71

Chapter 5—Scouting and Hunt Preparation 85

Part II: How to Hunt the Wild Turkey 101

Chapter 6—Spring Gobbler Hunting 103

Chapter 7—Hunting Fall Turkeys 127

Part III: The Complete Turkey Hunter 145

Chapter 8—Turkey Trophies and Tablefare 147

Chapter 9—Safety and Ethics in Turkey Hunting 159

Appendix 177

WELCOME TO TURKEY HUNTING

You might be on a misty Blue Ridge mountain when it hits you. It may be near the Colorado/New Mexico border, as the Sangre de Cristos awaken to spring. Or a spooky cypress swamp, fringe of a Midwestern pasture, or deep in the Vermont pines.

It could be almost anywhere, anytime, when you discover the common thread that binds the souls of all turkey hunters, the quiet joy and raw excitement that make turkey hunting not just sport but an addiction, a passion and obsession.

Is it the time of year, the thrill of a chilling gobble, or the heart-gripping suspense as a brassy tom turkey comes hunting you? Maybe it's just the beauty of that spectacular all-American bird, the fine trophy and tablefare.

Turkey hunting is made up of many elements. The art of calling a gobbler to the gun is the essence of turkey hunting, but there's much more than that.

Knowing the turkey's behavior and natural history is of prime importance. A turkey hunter must study the nature of his quarry—turkeys in general and the specific birds he hunts—to realize the most success and enjoyment from the sport. A knowledge of this fascinating bird shows you where and how to find turkeys, helps you plan hunting strategy, and enhances your appreciation of the animal beyond that of a hunter/prey relationship.

Woodsmanship skills are equally important. When a gobbler announces three ridges away, knowing how to get there and doing so quickly are more important than award-winning calling ability.

You also have to know guns, loads, and shooting. You've got to be geared up to get the most from your skills and to remain comfortable so you can hunt longer.

Musket-toting immigrants found the American turkey easy prey 350 years ago, but the big birds' descendents are much wiser today. They've evolved from the cagiest and hardiest birds—the ones that survived the relentless guns of hungry pioneers and greedy market hunters. Therefore, we descendents of those pilgrims must be equally shrewd, employing clever and creative hunting techniques. Tactics vary in different situations and depend on whether you are hunting spring or fall, or with decoys or dogs. And good calling is an important key to your wild turkey dinner.

Along with the recreation are the responsibilities: the safety, ethics, and conservation necessary to perpetuate the sport. Modern turkey hunting is a marvel of game and habitat management—made possible primarily by the efforts of dedicated outdoorsmen. With continued improvements in turkey populations and hunting ethics, the sport will get even better.

Turkey hunting today requires a lot of know-how. This book is designed to teach you those skills to make turkey hunting even more enjoyable and successful in years to come.

Photo by Charlie Farmer

Part I
Before the Hunt

CHAPTER 1

BIOLOGY AND BEHAVIOR OF THE WILD TURKEY

T he wild turkey's fascinating characteristics and natural history have made it one of the most sought game animals in North America. With keen senses and fabled intelligence, the elusive turkey can be the most challenging target a hunter may face, as well as a prize trophy. Knowing as much as possible about this unique bird will help you enjoy hunting to the utmost and give you the best chance for success.

Characteristics and Behavior

The American turkey is the largest species of gamebird on the continent, reaching more than 20 pounds with a wingspan of up to six feet. The forerunner of all domestic turkeys, the wild turkey resembles the bronze tame variety, each with iridescent and multicolored plumage that often appears black at a distance.

NRA Staff Photo

The regal wild turkey gobbler (left and center) is America's largest, most elusive gamebird. Hen turkeys (right), at about 10 pounds, are half the size of gobblers. Turkeys pictured are of the Eastern subspecies.

Wild turkeys appear more streamlined, with thinner bodies and longer neck, tail, wings, and legs than the barnyard type.

Mature males, called toms or gobblers, have a cluster of coarse, bristle-like feathers, called a beard, that hangs from the chest. In birds of the year, called jakes, the beard may be unapparent or only a couple inches long; older gobblers may have a beard—sometimes several—of a foot or longer. The beard grows throughout the tom's life but is kept short by breakage and abrasion. During spring hunting seasons, when hens are nesting and protected, the beard is one of the things a hunter looks for to identify a legal target.

Another characteristic of male turkeys is the bony "spur" that grows on the inside of each leg. It is used to fend off predators and to fight other toms during the mating season. Like the beard, it is insignificant on yearlings but becomes prominent with age. Spurs grow sharper and longer—to a maximum of about an inch and a half—as the tom grows older.

Hens, usually half the size of gobblers, occasionally grow beards and more rarely spurs, but can be distinguished from toms by their smaller bodies and lighter color. A hen's breast feathers are tipped with a band of brown or buff; a tom's feathers have sharp black borders and are darker and more iridescent

Photo by Roy E. Decker

A unique gamebird, the wild turkey gobbler is characterized by his beard, spurs, and warty folds of skin on his nearly bare head. When excited during breeding season, the gobbler's head turns bright red, white, and blue as part of his gaudy courtship ritual.

Turkey hens (1) can be distinguished at any time of year by their light-edged body feathers, more feathered heads and lack of spurs. Adult gobblers have a darker appearance resulting from black edged body feathers (2) and generally long beards and spurs. Even in their first fall, immature males, (3) have more colorful heads than hens, and button spurs. In spring, their tail fans often appear irregular while those of adult gobblers (4) are more symmetrical.

than those of a female. This makes the tom appear darker overall with a "polished" appearance.

The heads and necks of both sexes have wattles and caruncles—loose, warty projections of skin. Those of the female are much smaller and do not have the bright red, white, and blue coloration of the spring gobbler. The gobbler's head and neck are nearly bare of feathers. The hen's head appears bare, but is covered with short, hair-like feathers.

Vision and Hearing

The turkey's nervous system equips him well for survival. Like most birds, his intelligence ranks high in the animal kingdom. Keen eyesight—his best defense—allows him to pick up color, movement, contrast, and detail very quickly and accurately. Experiments have shown that turkeys react to slight changes in the color of a gobbler's head. They also can tell the difference between yellow and white corn. Turkey biologists differ on whether the eyesight of turkeys is much keener than man's, but it is generally accepted that turkeys see movement much better, and they perceive, analyze, and react to what they see much faster. A turkey, it is believed, can see in an instant what a man can see only after long and careful scanning. Tests show, however, that nocturnal vision in turkeys is not as good as in most mammals. Turkeys can see somewhat on moonlit nights, but not on dark nights. This makes their nighttime roosting behavior very important for survival.

Less research has been performed on the hearing of turkeys, though most biologists believe they can hear better than man. Experienced hunters know turkeys are attuned to even very subtle sounds that seem out of place. Turkeys have a very poor sense of smell, however. Scenting is probably not a factor in detecting predators, including human hunters.

Flocking and Roosting

Turkeys optimize their defenses by flocking together, with a half-dozen or more pairs of eyes and ears monitoring surroundings as they travel together. In summer, these flocks consist mainly of family units—a hen and her brood of young, called poults. In late summer and fall these units merge with others to form larger flocks of hens and birds of the year, while mature males generally keep to themselves in flocks, the flock size depending on population density. Gobblers, hens, and young come together just before spring breeding season and soon break into flocks of a single dominant gobbler and his harem of hens. Usu-

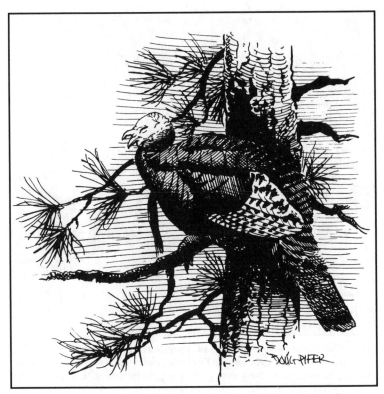

Roosting trees provide nighttime safety for turkeys when they are unable to use their best defense–their eyesight. While turkeys have unequalled vision, they lack the nocturnal sight of their predators.

ally there are four to six hens in a flock, and there may also be a subordinate male turkey or two. Occasionally the breeding flock may be only one gobbler and one hen, or a flock of a dozen or more hens with two or more strutting, breeding toms.

For protection when nightfall nullifies their best defense, turkeys roost in trees, out of reach of most predators. When danger does threaten on the ground, they may fly at 55 mph, run at 18 mph, or occasionally fight with beaks and spurs.

Turkey Subspecies

All American turkeys are of the species *Meleagris gallopavo*, which is divided into several subspecies, each with slightly different physical and behavioral characteristics. The subspecies are adapted to different types of habitat that occur in different regions, but there is considerable overlap of the subspecies.

7

Photo by Irene Vandermolen, Leonard Rue Enterprises

While the turkey's main mode of transportation is walking, the big birds fly well when they must. Turkeys prefer to soar downhill when making an escape so they can glide long distances with little effort.

The varying characteristics conform to the biological laws of natural selection. These principles state that warm-blooded animals living farther north or south of the equator will be larger with shorter extremities than their counterparts in temperate zones, and that those living in the darker, moister habitats will be the darkest in coloration. These adaptations help protect animals through heat conservation in the first instance and through camouflage in the second. There are other regional adaptations.

M.g. silvestris, commonly called the Eastern turkey, is the most widely distributed, abundant, and hunted turkey subspecies. Since it ranges the farthest north, it can also grow to be among the largest; toms average 18 to 20 pounds, with hens weighing about half that. Old, northern birds may occasionally approach 30 pounds. *Silvestris* inhabits the hardwood and mixed forests from New England and southern Canada to northern Florida and west to Texas, Missouri, Iowa, and Minnesota. It has also been successfully transplanted in California and Oregon. The Eastern turkey is characterized by its large size and rich, bronze-colored body feathers and chestnut-brown tailfeather tips. Their

The most widely distributed and abundant subspecies is the Eastern wild turkey, distinguished from others by its large, bronze-colored body and chestnut tailfeather tips.

brown, black, and white barred wings can stretch over five feet from tip to tip.

M.g. osceola, or the Florida turkey, is the subspecies native to the Florida peninsula. There is a smaller distribution in southern Georgia, Louisiana, and other southeastern states. Where the ranges of *osceola* and *silvestris* overlap, birds show characteristics of both subspecies and can be difficult to distinguish.

The true *osceola* is smaller than the Eastern turkey, darker in color, and has less white barring in the wing quills. Its feathers

Similar to the Eastern turkey, the *osceola* turkey is a bit smaller and darker in color. Also called the Florida turkey, *osceola* has the smallest range of any turkey subspecies.

9

are more iridescent green and red, with less bronze than *silvestris*. The bird's coloration and behavior are adapted to the flat pine woods, oak and palmetto hammocks, and swamps of the South.

M.g. intermedia is native to the brushy scrub country of the southern Great Plains, South Texas, and Mexico, where it got its common name, Rio Grande turkey. This subspecies has a body size similar to *osceola*, and slightly longer legs. The birds are comparatively pale and copper colored. They inhabit brushy areas near streams or mesquite pine and scrub oak forests. The Rio Grande turkey may be found up to 6,000 feet above sea level, and generally favors country that is more open than the

Photo by Luther Goldman, U.S. Fish and Wildlife Service

Light tips on its tail and tail covert feathers, as well as a paler overall appearance, sets the Rio Grande turkey apart from its Eastern cousin.

habitat favored by its eastern counterparts. In some areas, it has distinct summer and winter ranges. Intermedia has been successfully transplanted in areas of greatly differing habitat, from northern Idaho to Hawaii.

M.g. merriami, or Merriam's turkey, lives in the pine and hardwood forests of the western mountains and plains, from Montana and Washington to northern Arizona. A population is also growing in eastern Minnesota. Its size is comparable to the Eastern turkey, but it is blacker with blue, purple, and bronze reflections. Merriam's appears to have a white rump due to its pink, buff, or white tail coverts and tail tips. These tailfeather tips are very conspicuous when the strutting gobbler is against a dark background.

Photo Courtesy New Mexico Game and Fish Department

Merriam's turkey of the western U.S. has conspicuous white markings on its wings and tail. Densest populations are in Colorado, Wyoming, and the Dakotas.

Another turkey subspecies occurs in southwestern United States, *M.g. mexicana* or Gould's turkey of northern and central Mexico. Gould's turkey, ranges into Arizona and New Mexico and is the largest of all subspecies. There are huntable populations of Gould's turkeys found in scattered wild regions of the Southwest.

Habitat Needs

The turkey is a tough animal with well-developed survival skills. Some have been known to live for more than three weeks without food. They thrive in harsh regions—from the cold and snow of Quebec to the arid plateaus of Arizona; the steamy jungles of Mexico's Yucatan Peninsula to the mile-high Rockies of Wyoming.

Despite their adaptability, there seems to be one constant in turkey habitat that all subspecies prefer. That is a mature or semi-mature forest with rich mast foods, safe roosting sites, and occasional open cover that lets the birds use their eyesight to detect danger from afar.

This habitat comes in the form of mixed forests of conifers (pine, cedar, cypress, and hemlock) and hardwoods (beech, oak, maple, gum, etc.). Roosting areas are often found in stands of white pine, tupelo, or cypress in the East, and ponderosa pine

Photo Courtesy Missouri Dept. of Conservation   *Photo by Luther Goldman, USFWS*

Wild turkeys have evolved into separate subspecies to cope with various types of habitat. While the Eastern turkey thrives best in hardwood forests (left), the Rio Grande adapts well to the more arid, open areas of the Southwest (right).

in the West. Even when encountering *intermedia* in the scrublands or prairie of the Southwest, you can be assured there is at least one good roosting site nearby. It may be a telephone pole.

Though they were found virtually everywhere during colonial times, Eastern turkeys seem to prefer rugged mountainous habitat or big ridges. The reason is that big, mature forests are now often in rugged country; many flatland forests have long-since been turned to cropland or otherwise developed. A dense human population and good accessibility to hunting areas has also led to great hunting pressure in the East, and the most rugged areas see the least pressure. Finally, inhabiting a high ridge allows turkeys to fly up and glide across a valley a mile or more away—offering them a no-nonsense means of escape. Turkeys are, however, increasing throughout the eastern piedmont country and other flatland areas where habitat is improving. They are often found in swamps and have adapted to areas of mixed timber and cropland. Some of the densest turkey populations now occur in woodlots and river bottoms in agricultural areas.

Western turkeys often face the problem of finding sufficent water. A constant source of surface water is essential to turkey survival, and is a prime limiting factor for the Rio Grande and Merriam's turkeys. Conversely, hunters of those subspecies know that concentrations of turkeys may be found around the scarce springs or waterholes.

Another universal habitat requirement is forest openings such as meadows, swamps, clearcuts, logging roads, rights of way, and fields. These areas produce and attract large quantities of insects, which are the staple food of newly hatched poults. Insects provide the protein necessary for the energy needs and rapid growth of poults. Though the woods provide most food for adult turkeys, the cool shadows of the deep forest harbor few bugs for poults.

In large forests, occasional openings such as powerline rights of way are very beneficial to turkeys, providing insects vital to the nutritional requirements of poults.

Wild Turkey Foods

Turkeys eat a variety of foods depending on season, habitat, and availablity. Their appetite is so diverse that up to 60 different food items have been found in a single turkey crop examined by biologists.

In spring, adult turkeys also prefer insects, along with new green sprouts and buds. (The toms, however, eat little during spring mating season. Preoccupied with breeding, fighting, and chasing hens, toms live mainly off large fat reserves stored in its body in an area called the breast sponge.)

As summer arrives turkeys continue to eat insects, especially grasshoppers, along with soft fruits, mushrooms, grains, and green plants. Their diets may change weekly as summer turns to autumn and different foods ripen. Acorns are the staple fall and winter food for many turkeys across the continent, but turkeys also eat beechnuts, wild grapes, dogwoods, and other fruits and nuts, as well as wild and cultivated grains.

Peak feeding times are generally the first couple hours after the birds come off roost in the morning, and the last couple hours of daylight. Like many gamebirds, however, turkeys may roost for days at a time without feeding during harsh weather or when there is deep snow.

Winter can mean lean and hard times for turkeys, especially in northern zones where winterkill can occasionally take a fourth of the population. They seek spring seeps where ground does not freeze; there they are able to scratch up acorns, aquatic plants and animals, tubers, roots, seeds, and sometimes carrion. Turkeys have little difficulty with three or four inches of light snow and mild weather, but are unable to dig through deep snow or hard-frozen ground. During this time, however, their competitive relationship with deer may reverse; turkeys may glean leavings in areas pawed up by deer. In harsh weather turkeys may also consume such emergency food items as pine and hemlock needles, buds, lichens, and moss.

Communication

Turkeys have a complex social system and communicate through sight and sound. Their flocking behavior, coupled with good communication, makes them elusive prey for predators, including man. But sometimes those defenses can backfire. Hunters who know how and when to hide from or stimulate a turkey's senses can turn them against the bird and use them as effective hunting techniques.

Wild turkeys have a wide array of calls to send a variety of messages. Over two dozen different calls, falling into a handful of categories, have been identified by researchers.

It is believed that a turkey can communicate even before it is hatched; poults begin peeping while still inside their eggs, ensuring they receive motherly attention. The nesting hen, in turn, responds with a hoot-like call. This establishes an early bond with her young and may prompt the poults to hatch at about the same time.

Photo by Leonard Lee Rue III

The most brazen form of turkey communication, the gobble is used by male turkeys to challenge other toms, attract hens, or simply let off steam. It is most common during the spring breeding season, but may be heard any time of year.

The yelp is the most common turkey call. It begins as a peep made by poults to keep the family together and evolves into several calls, all variations on the theme, "Here I am, where are you?" This information is useful to turkeys when flocks become scattered and want to regroup, when roosting turkeys want others to know they're ready to fly down in the morning, and in many other situations.

When poults become separated from the brood or otherwise distressed, they emit high whistles to alert their mother. As the poult grows into an adult, these whistles develop into the "kee-kee-run" yelp of a lost turkey. This is the call most often used by hunters to attract turkeys in the fall.

Turkeys also have a repertoire of clucks and cutts they use for "conversation" as they move together in flocks. When feeding, members of a flock give a soft purring sound, a call that denotes contentment or establishes a turkey's own personal space. If another should invade that space, the turkey will purr louder or make a raspy, threatening cackle. A turkey looking for a flock to join with gives the "cutt" call. Not to be confused with the melodious three-note kee-kee-run, the cutt is a long, loud series of clucks.

The most dramatic and well-known turkey call is the adult tom's bold, intimidating gobble. The wild turkey gobble, booming through a bare forest at twilight, is the trademark of the spring mating season.

Breeding Season

Interaction among turkeys increases dramatically with the onset of spring and the breeding season. Flocks of hens and gobblers begin to mix, toms wage verbal and physical battle for the ladies' attention, and new breeding flocks are created.

Lengthening periods of daylight in spring trigger a hormone increase in turkeys that initiates breeding behavior. The time of this occurrence varies according to elevation and latitude, but is in March (February to May) over most of the turkey's range.

The breeding season begins with lone bachelors or flocks of toms getting the urge for female companionship, and they join with hens after a long year of separation. Flocks during this season may be only a handful of birds or dozens, and may contain many gobblers. Both sexes begin early courtship behavior, becoming very vocal. Toms begin to gobble and strut, but haven't started to breed hens or fight other males.

Photo by Ron Keil, Ohio Department of Natural Resources

At the onset of breeding season, toms begin to strut, tipping their bodies horizontally, fanning their tails, and dragging their wing tips. This ritual makes them appear bigger and stronger—a way of intimidating rivals and charming the ladies.

As mating commences, the older toms begin chasing off younger birds and establishing territories prior to gathering hens. They announce their intentions to the world with loud and frequent gobbling. Gobbling is meant to establish territories, warn or challenge other gobblers in the area, and attract hens. This is the peak gobbling period, a brief but intense time when toms often sound off all day long. The fired-up toms are always on edge, and gobble at nearly any sound: crows, owls, even train whistles and slamming car doors.

Once a dominant male has kicked out the competition and claimed a territory and harem of receptive hens, gobbling decreases. A tom does most of his gobbling right after waking up, to assert his presence and locate members of his harem before flying down in the morning. Gobbling decreases throughout the morning, and is very sparce in the afternoon. Gobblers usually let loose briefly, however, just before going up to their roost at sunset, or when they hear a hen call or disturbing sound. Particularly lonely or lusty toms may gobble all day.

Harems
During this period, gobblers are usually receptive to a new hen that might become available, but don't go out of their way to recruit new mates. They devote most of their time to servicing

17

and supervising their existing harem. Toms show dominance and stimulate hens to mate through a gaudy courtship ritual of swelling and strutting. A strutting tom tips his body horizontally, drops his wings, and raises his tail vertically into a broad fan. He fluffs his body feathers and spreads his tail almost 180 degrees while pulling his head in close. As he first breaks into strut, dragging his wing tips stiffly across the ground, he emits a deep hissing sound from his throat. When the dominant tom struts near other males, it usually inhibits them from going into full strut. If it doesn't, a spur-slashing, beak-pecking fight may break out, ending with the loser scurrying into the woods and the winner strutting bigger than ever. Whipped toms and jakes are afraid to gobble or emit only feeble combinations of gobbles and yelps. They can do very little breeding in the presence of the boss gobbler.

After laying their clutch of a dozen eggs, hens spend the next month on their nest. If the eggs are destroyed during incubation, the hen may lay a new clutch without rebreeding.

Toms normally spend the day with the harem during peak breeding season, strutting and mating through the day. Hens slip away individually to lay an egg. Toms follow hens as the flock travels, but call stray hens near by gobbling. Mating becomes regular, and each hen lays one egg per day, for a total of about a dozen eggs. As the breeding season comes to a close, however, most hens have been bred and are nesting. When the last mate disappears for good, the distraught, lonesome tom goes into another gobbling peak, which lasts several days.

Nesting

If a nest is destroyed by predators, flood, or other cause, hens may lay a second or third clutch of eggs without remating. There were theories that toms destroy all eggs they can find, trying to prolong mating, but most biologists discard the belief today.

After an incubation period of about 28 days, poults hatch with full abilities to see and run. They immediately begin eating insects, instinctively pecking at any small object that moves. Predators are especially dangerous in the two to three weeks before poults learn to fly. When they are very young, poults depend on the remnants of their yolk sac for nourishment and the cover of their mother's wing for protection from the elements. But a couple weeks after hatching, with yolk reserves gone and too large for the hen to cover, they face the perils of starvation and

Photo by Leonard Lee Rue III

Immediately after hatching, turkey poults begin dashing about and pecking at insects. They learn to fly in two or three weeks.

exposure. They are most vulnerable to pneumonia when cold rains soak their light down. In years of prolonged cold and rain in spring, nearly the entire crop of poults may be lost in some areas.

Very young poults find protection from the elements beneath their mother's wing. Later, they become too large to gather there, and are vulnerable to sickness after exposure to cold rains.

Wild Turkeys and Man

Turkeys and humans have had a stormy relationship through the ages. Indians depended on the birds as a food source for hundreds of years, as did the early settlers from Europe. But then legions of land developers, pioneers, and hunters destroyed habitat and entire flocks, driving the wild turkey to the brink of disaster in much of its range. Turkeys then became dependent on man for recovery through harvest and habitat management. But now this relationship has finally culminated in the best possible situation: conscientious sportsmen who place as much importance in conservation as a successful hunt, and a well-adapted, expanding breed of turkey that provides those conservationist-hunters with the ultimate hunting challenge.

Prehistoric Times

The wild turkey was important to native Americans long before recorded history. Expansive forests harbored ample flocks of a rather dull-witted breed of bird—one that had little need for cunning because of the light hunting pressure. Fossils show they were hunted and even domesticated by Indians in the East and Southwest. Turkey bones 15,000-50,000 years old have been found in caves and streambeds used by Indians in what is now Pennsylvania, Kentucky, Arkansas, New Mexico, Indiana, Illinois, and Florida.

Turkeys were a frequent menu item as well as source of clothing, ornaments, and even weapons. Eastern woodland Indians wove turkey feathers into garments and used them to fletch arrows. They even tipped their arrows with the spurs from gobblers. Bones were fashioned into awls, beads, and spoons, while the bright feathers adorned headbands, ceremonial garments, and hunting tools. Recently uncovered southwestern Indian pottery, dating from the year 1,000, is decorated with depictions of turkeys.

When Spanish explorers first arrived in Mexico they found turkeys domesticated by the Aztec Indians. The first turkeys to appear in Europe were brought back by these explorers around 1520. At that time, Europeans were also learning of other exotic birds, such as the guinea fowl and peacock, and there was confusion over the identity of these three birds. The name "turkey" was probably coined by Europeans who believed the bird came from that country. The turkey's scientific name, *Meleagris gallopavo*, comes from three Latin words meaning guinea hen, chicken, and pea fowl.

Colonial Times

Domesticated turkeys from continental Europe were introduced to England, where several varieties were developed and exported all over the world. Domestic turkeys brought to the early American colonies were smaller and darker, with different markings on the tail feathers, than the native birds colonists encountered.

The wild turkey was a revered American resource from the earliest days. Ben Franklin, whose judgment was among the most respected of any colonists, had this to say of the turkey in his *Poor Richard's Almanack*:

> *I wish the bald eagle had not been chosen as the representative of our country; he is a bird of bad moral character. The turkey is in comparison a much more reputable bird and a true, original native of America. Eagles have been found*

21

in all countries, but the turkey was peculiar to ours. He is (though a little vain and silly...) a bird of courage and would not hesitate to attack a grenadier of the British guard, who should presume to invade his farmyard.

Mr. Franklin would be pleased to know that in the minds of many sportsmen 200 years later, the turkey would indeed be a symbol of what they loved most about America.

Photo Courtesy Arkansas Game and Fish Commission

Unrestricted hunting and habitat destruction eliminated the turkey over much of its range by the early 1900s. Forest regrowth and a more responsible attitude toward wildlife have helped the turkeys flourish again in recent years.

Early hunters pursued the turkey for strictly selfish reasons, however. Settlers seldom turned down the opportunity to put turkey on the table. The relatively easy prey was eliminated from the mid-Atlantic region, and eventually pioneers and market hunters permeated the turkey's range. Turkey populations were decimated from uncontrolled hunting and land-clearing and timbering practices that leveled the virgin forests vital to their livelihood. By the early 1900s, turkeys survived only in wilderness regions of Florida, South Carolina, Alabama, Mississippi, Texas, and scattered areas in the West and Northeast.

This was a time of awakening on the part of sportsmen, however, and their attitudes quickly changed. They realized that the seemingly endless supply of game was hardly that, and wildlife was indeed a vulnerable, disappearing resource. Something had to be done. Hunting seasons were cancelled or severely restricted, and people began to realize wildlife management was possible and necessary.

Early attempts to restore turkeys involved releasing birds raised in captivity. These efforts failed, however, because pen-reared turkeys are usually not hardy enough to survive, breed, and expand their populations. Occasionally these released birds wandered into barnyards and bred with domestic turkeys, which further weakened the wild stock and exposed it to diseases. Later efforts to breed wild gobblers with wing-clipped, pen-raised hens also proved ineffective.

Photo Courtesy Arkansas Game and Fish Comm.

Photo Courtesy Illinois Dept. of Conservation

Photo by Ron Keil, Ohio D.N.R.

Attempting to establish new populations of wild turkeys, early wildlife managers first tried releasing pen-raised birds. Those efforts failed, but trapping and release of wild turkeys to new areas has proven very successful. The wild turkey's range is now much larger than it was originally.

But in the mid-1900s wildlife management became a serious science, and concerned sportsmen provided funding to make sure it was used for practical applications. Wildlife managers found new methods for trapping large numbers of wild turkeys. They then reintroduced the birds to areas that had good habitat but no native population, and the turkeys flourished.

By the 1950s, turkeys were re-established in dozens of regions in several states where they had disappeared a half-century before. In Pennsylvania, for example, turkeys had been virtually exterminated in the northern half of the state by the 1930s. But an intensive 15-year restoration effort, along with natural expansion of the southern turkey population, culminated in a turkey hunting season in 1954 that saw 15,000 birds taken in the northern region. Today, turkeys are hunted statewide with an annual harvest of over 35,000 birds.

Elsewhere, forests regrew naturally, habitat was enhanced, turkey transplant projects continued, and research progressed— mainly due to license fees and excise taxes paid by hunters. In the meantime, the hardy, intelligent bird evolved into a canny, elusive, and adaptable animal. Turkeys hunted today are descendants of the smartest and most elusive of the species—those that escaped the ordeals that wiped out lesser individuals.

Turkeys Today

Today, these factors have combined to restore the turkey to its former range and more: All states but Alaska now have turkeys and the total population is over 4.5 million. They now live even in areas that were originally unfit for turkey habitation. For example, in some of the arid regions of the Southwest, the cover could support turkeys but there is a severe scarcity of surface water. The installation of "guzzlers," which collect rainwater in an underground reservoir and release it to the surface slowly, has made thousands of acres of arid land suitable for the species. Turkeys of various subspecies have found the living fine in Idaho, Montana, California, Hawaii, and other states where there were no turkeys originally.

Photo by Joe Workosky

Turkey hunters today enjoy the best sport in nearly a century. Bird populations are growing and expanding well beyond their original range, thanks to forest growth, advanced wildlife management programs, and contributions by hunters and other conservationists.

Long-term turkey management techniques include planting food plots, burning or bulldozing forest openings, and maintaining forest roads and rights of way as feeding areas for turkey flocks. Spot feeding of wild turkeys is generally not considered a good management technique. Some biologists believe it may be of limited benefit in deep snow conditions; others believe it does more harm than good.

State game departments continually collect data on the age and condition of turkeys through live trapping and examination of harvested birds. The studies help them learn more about behavior, nutrition, and disease in the species.

Through natural forest regrowth, coupled with research and management, turkeys have recovered dramatically and continue to increase their range. New record harvests in several states occur each year, indicating increasing populations. Several other states have just started or greatly expanded turkey hunting in the last decade, as flocks have gained a foothold.

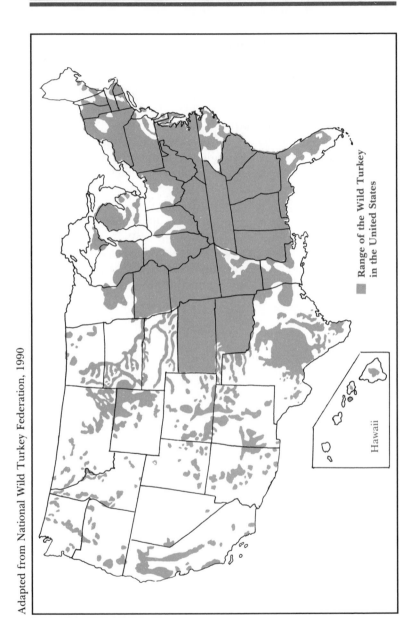

Adapted from National Wild Turkey Federation, 1990

Range of the Wild Turkey
in the United States

Hawaii

CHAPTER 2
TURKEY CALLS AND CALLING

Photo by Mike Strandlund

To most turkey hunters, calling a bird into shotgun range is the name of the game. Mastering yelps and clucks on a simple call like this peg and slate will lure birds, but it's best to have a comprehensive knowledge of turkey calls and calling.

F or most hunters, calling birds to the gun is the essence of turkey hunting. The thrill lies in busting a flock, then convincing hesitant turkeys to return. Or in seducing a hot gobbler, hearing him warily approach, and finally watching the brilliant bird, completely fooled, strut into gun range in courtship of you!

Calling turkeys is one of the oldest arts practiced in North America. Thousand-year-old etchings on cave walls depict Indians luring turkeys with their voices. They were also inventors of crude peg-and-slate calls, wingbone yelpers, and decoys—forerunners of modern calls and lures.

Today, turkey calling is a multimillion-dollar business, with over 200 manufacturers making thousands of different calls and instructional tapes for hunters eager to master the talk of the turkey. There are seemingly endless calls to choose from and a mind-boggling array of sounds you need to make to call turkeys.

Is all this calling hoopla necessary? Yes and no. Calling is often overrated. Some would have us believe that only contest-quality callers can consistently lure birds. This simply isn't so; while a precise and diverse vocabulary is helpful, most turkeys are called in with only a few discreet clucks or yelps. And turkeys, after all, have voices as varied as humans. Then again, some wise old birds will respond only to a certain call or a certain caller. The secret is to know when, where, and which of the basic calls to use. Then, through experience and experiment, learn to expand your turkey language for effective calling in any situation.

Calls to Learn

The basic calls to learn are the yelp and cluck. Turkeys can be taken in both spring and fall with only these two calls. The cackle, purr, kee-kee run, and gobble are more advanced calls that can help you bag the smart old birds that need extra persuasion. There are other calls recognized by experts, but they are generally variations or a combination of the basic calls.

Yelp

The yelp is a call wild turkeys use in a variety of situations. In most cases, however, it is made by turkeys trying to locate or associate with others. In spring, hens yelp to let the gobblers know where they are. In autumn, hens yelp to collect their brood. Gobblers yelp less often than hens, and usually limit their yelping to the fall when they are trying to find a lost buddy. Many calls can reproduce a gobbler yelp and all calls can produce a hen yelp.

Typically, hen turkeys yelp in a series of about five soft notes, often preceded by a whine, which sounds like "yoke-yoke-yoke-yoke-yoke..." Some callers consider the yelp to be a two-syllable sound, pronounced "kee-yoke." There are variations on the yelp—yelps of a lost turkey are 10 to 20 louder and raspier calls, while the tree yelp, made from the roost at first light, are only two or three barely audible notes.

In using the yelp call, remember that turkeys yelp sparingly. If they dashed through the woods yelping constantly, as some hunters seem to think, every predator in the forest would have them pinpointed. Keep your yelps to a minimum.

Turkeys are very vocal, conversing as they feed together, calling when they're apart, and scolding if others crowd too close. Their dozens of calls have specific meanings; to call turkeys, you need to learn their language.

Cluck and Putt

The turkey's cluck may express contentment or questioning. When feeding, turkeys cluck to communicate reassurance that all is well with the flock. The cluck is also used by a bird trying to regroup with the flock. When clucking, make only one or two at a time and try to sound "content;" this minimizes the chance your call will be mistaken for an alarm putt. Sharp, quick "putts" (very similar to a cluck but more urgent and quick) are made by a frightened turkey. Take care not to duplicate this sound, or nearby turkeys will quickly disperse. Clucks can be made successfully with just about every type of call.

Whistle or Kee-Kee Run

This is the name given to the call of a lost young bird. Kee-kee squeals, followed by yelps or clucks, usually indicate the turkey is lost or separated from its flock and is anxious to rejoin.

The kee-kee run is a whining, whistling series of "kees" and yelps. The call usually sounds like "kee-kee-kee-yelp-yelp," though the yelps and kees may be made in any order. While the cluck should sound relaxed, so it is not confused with a putt, the kee-kee run should sound panicky.

This call is most effective in fall but can occasionally be used

The panicky squeals and yelps of a bird of the year are known as kee-kee runs. It is the call most often used by hunters to attract turkeys in fall.

with success during the spring. It is all but impossible to duplicate on a friction call, but it can be reproduced easily on a diaphragm or tube call.

Cackle

The cackle is a series of very fast, urgent, high-pitched clucks, usually preceded and followed by several regular, though sharp, yelps. The cackle starts at a slow rate and low pitch, slides up to a higher note and speed, then back down. The most common use of the cackle is to announce a turkey is going to fly down from the roost or is preparing to take flight from the ground. The sound is similar to "yoke-yoke-*yo-y-y-y-y-yo*-yoke-yoke- yoke."

Some experts believe hens cackle only at takeoff, but others believe there is sometimes a mating cackle. At any rate, gobblers often seem to be turned on by a persistent cackle when nothing else works.

Several types of calling devices can make the cackle, but the diaphragm usually works best.

Purr

Purrs are another form of turkey conversation. They are an even-pitch, drawn-out call of the same tone of a cluck or yelp, which sounds like "purrrrr..." They are usually used in combination with clucks or yelps.

Turkey callers usually use a purr as a variety call secondary to clucks or yelps, just to mix up their repertoire a bit. It is also a quiet call used to lure a gobbler the final few steps.

Cutt

The cutt is a rapid, irregular string of clucks that vary in pitch. It is usually made by turkeys looking for company or an aggressive hen trying to get a gobbler's attention. This call sounds like "*cut*...cut-*cut*...cut.....cut."

Because cutts sound very similar to alarm putts, they should only be attempted by accomplished callers.

Gobble

The gobble is the trademark of male turkeys in spring, used to attract hens and intimidate enemies or rivals. Though its applications are limited, it can be helpful to hunters.

The wild turkey gobble is an explosion of over a dozen individual notes lasting two to four seconds. Gobbles of mature birds sound powerful and confident. Subordinate toms and jakes have a gobble that sounds weak and self-conscious. Either type of gobble is among the most difficult turkey call for the hunter to master, but even a decent gobble can be enough to draw a re-

Gobbling helps toms get their way, but it also makes them vulnerable to hunters. The gobble of mature birds has a confident ring; jakes and subordinate toms usually gobble little.

sponse from a jealous spring tom ready to fight for his turf. Turkeys can also be fooled into gobbling in fall, but much less frequently.

Most hunters make gobbles with special gobbling tubes or with box calls, though they can also be made with diaphragms and other devices.

Gobbles are used for locating toms and enticing hesitant turkeys into coming closer. They must be used with great discretion, however, because they also draw hunters who think your gobbling comes from a real turkey. Gobbling will scare off subordinate toms and jakes in spring.

Calling Devices

Hunters who understand the meaning of turkey language — when, where, and how it should be used — have won half the battle in talking turkeys to the gun. A few talented callers can do it with only their voices or maybe a piece of grass held to their lips. The vast majority, however, rely on calling devices.

Turkey calls are like musical instruments. They range in design from concert violins to children's toy horns. The skill needed to play them is just as varied. And the quality of music they put forth is equal to the quality of the instrument and the amount of talent and practice time the player has invested.

There are two basic types of calls: those that produce sound by friction, and those that operate by moving air through an

Photo by Mike Strandlund

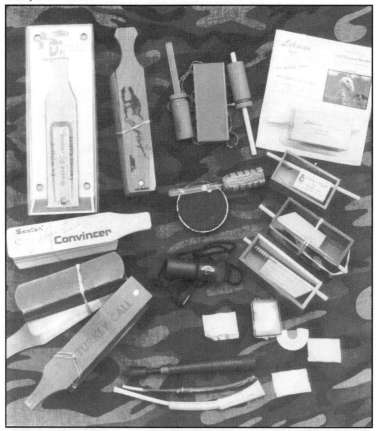

With dozens of designs and hundreds of brands to choose from, turkey calls have a variety of purposes and features. A hunter should try out different types to see which is most practical and which produces the best sound for him.

orifice or over a diaphragm. Many variations exist within these two types and each type has advantages and disadvantages.

Air-Operated Turkey Calls

Air-operated calls duplicate turkey sounds when the caller causes air to flow into, over, or through the call. Diaphragms, tubes, snuffboxes, and wingbones are the most prevalent air-operated calls today.

33

Diaphragm

The diaphragm mouth call has recently become the most popular turkey call. It is a small, horseshoe-shaped yoke with one or more thin latex strips stretched across the opening. The call is held against the roof of the mouth by tongue pressure. Sound is controlled by the tongue's placement on the diaphragm, the configuration of the mouth, and regulation of air pressure. Diaphragms are made in a variety of designs and can be manipulated many ways, enabling the caller to make soft or loud varieties of

Photo by Mike Strandlund

Photo Courtesy Missouri Dept. of Conservation

The inside-the mouth diaphragm has become the most popular turkey call. Good diaphragm users can simulate virtually any turkey call without movement and direct the sound away from their position. This call is inexpensive but has a short life.

virtually any turkey call. Some have multiple rubber strips that help the caller make calls that change pitch.

Not everyone can use a mouth diaphragm. Those with dental work, odd palate shapes, or uncontrollable gagging problems may not be able to use this call. Some hunters simply can't master the technique.

Those who do master the diaphragm can produce very realistic calls. A yelp is produced by saying words like "chee-uck" or "tee-uck" without using the vocal cords. With the word "puck," a good cluck can be achieved. A cackle is made with the word "tuck," beginning slow, speeding up to a very fast tempo, then slowing again.

Mouth-operated diaphragms, of course, are worked without use of the hands; this reduces hunter movement to an absolute minimum.

Tube Calls

The tube call is a diaphragm operated outside the mouth. It does away with the problems people have with standard diaphragm calls. Tube calls are capable of both very loud and very soft sounds. And all turkey sounds can be made with it, including gobbles.

Commercial tube-type calls are usually cylindrically shaped. They are made of a variety of materials and are approximately one to 1½ inches in diameter and two to four inches long. The mouthpiece is a half-circle with a thin rubber diaphragm stretched over the opening. The other end has a round hole about a half-inch in diameter, or it may be completely open to allow more air flow.

To use the call, place the lower lip on the mouthpiece. Roll the bottom lip into the upper half (cutout area), which contains the diaphragm. Force air onto the reed to produce a squealing sound. By "huffing" air from the throat and saying "her-row," you can produce a yelp. Dropping the jaw as you say "row" will make a better yelp. Remember not to voice the words, but simply let air flow work the call.

A disadvantage of tubes is they require at least one hand to operate. In practice, they are operated by holding them to the mouth with one hand; the other hand may be moved over the end to vary the sound.

Wingbone

The wingbone or quill call may date back farther than any other type. Adult hen turkey wing bones are usually best for making authentic wingbone-type calls. Use two or three wing bones, inserted into each other, so the smallest one provides the mouthpiece orifice and the largest forms the bell, or sound chamber.

Commercial calls of this type are made from a very thin tube with a small hole in one end. The other end flairs open. The small end opening is only about ⅛-inch in diameter. The large end opening is about ¾-inch, and the call is six to eight inches long. These calls are made of plastic, rubber, wood, or metal, but a straw can be substituted in an emergency.

Turkey sounds are reproduced by pursing the lips and sucking air sharply through the smaller end of the instrument. Some find these calls difficult to use. When mastered, they produce a distinctive tone that sounds particularly true at a distance.

Friction Calls

Friction calls make turkey sounds when their parts are rubbed or scraped together. These parts are made of wood, slate, plastic, or metal and are worked by hand.

Hinged-Lid Box

The hinged-lid box call is a long-time favorite and the second-most popular turkey call today. The box produces some of the truest turkey calls. Also, box calls are relatively easy to master. Sound is produced when the wooden, chalked lid is scraped across the top edges of an enclosed sound chamber, or topless box.

Box calls can be made from any kind of wood, but mahogany, cedar, walnut, poplar, and cherry are most common. Calls produce various tones depending on the grain and type of wood. Harder woods generally produce higher-pitched sounds, while softwoods produce deeper sounds. Box calls are easily mastered and produce all turkey sounds except the whistle and kee-kee run. To operate, stroke the sides of the call with the lid, or paddle, in a forehand or backhand motion. This will produce a

Top Right
The box call, responsible for the demise of more turkeys than any other calling device, has been used for decades. It is easy to master, but requires hand motion to operate and needs care in wet weather.

Bottom Right
Hinged-lid boxes need more maintenance than most other types of turkey calls. They must be secured to keep from "squawking" in your pocket, and should be carried and operated in a plastic bag in damp weather. Box calls must be chalked periodically and kept hidden when you're calling a bird in close.

scratching sound much like the yelp of a turkey. To make a cluck, hold the paddle lightly against the box and tap it to one side. You can gobble with a box call by securing it with a rubber band (not too tight) and shaking it.

The hinged-lid box has some disadvantages: It is large, rather fragile, and noisy if improperly carried. It also requires special handling when used in damp or rainy weather. To protect a box call from moisture, carry and operate it in a plastic bag.

Scratch Box

The scratch box is smaller than the hinged-lid box. It too is capable of making very realistic turkey sounds. Because the striking surfaces are separate from each other, it is easier to carry and not as prone to making accidental noises as the hinged-lid box. It is more difficult to use than the hinged-lid box, however, as the angles and movements are not mechanically controlled and the striking surfaces can be misaligned.

Like the hinged-lid box, the scratch box is also incapable of the kee-kee. Both boxes can make either soft or loud calls. The main disadvantage of these two types of box calls is that they require two hands to operate.

Pushbutton Call

A relatively new type of call, designed mainly for beginners or box call users who want to minimize movement, is the pushbutton

Photo by Mike Strandlund

Pushbutton calls have two advantages: They are quick and easy to learn, and can be operated with very little movement. Some hunters attach pushbutton calls to their gunstocks so they can call while in shooting position.

call. With these mechanical calls, the striker is prepositioned against a plate within a sound box. Most are operated by holding the box in one hand and pushing a prealigned peg with the index finger. Many variations of this call exist. They have wood, slate, or plastic striking surfaces. The kee-kee run and the gobble are virtually impossible to produce on these calls, and it is more difficult to control tone and pitch than with other calls.

A hunter who can't operate a diaphragm but wants to call a bird close may tape a pushbutton call to his gunstock. This enables him to hide his movement and call with his gun in shooting position.

Grooved Calls

Like the pushbutton calls, the grooved calls are easy for novices to operate and produce acceptable sounds with very little practice. The most popular design is an aluminum plate mounted in a sounding box. A wooden or plastic peg is drawn along the plate to produce the sounds. Yelps and clucks are easy to make, but this device too is limited in the calls it can produce.

Peg-and-Slate/Glass/Aluminum

The slate friction call consists of two parts—the slate, glass or aluminum and the peg or striker. The slate is glued into a holder or simply cupped in the hand. There are fixed and adjustable slates. With a plexiglass striker point, the call is waterproof—a tremendous advantage on damp or rainy days. Peg-and-slate calls emit some of the most realistic turkey sounds.

To produce a yelp, scrape the striker head on the slate surface at an angle of about 45 degrees, pointed toward your body. The striker should not be lifted from the surface of the slate, but moved in short strokes for the cluck or circular motions for the yelp. To purr, drag the striker across the slate. An abrasive pad is included with most slates to keep it clean and rough, or you can use sandpaper.

A slate call is easy to operate, but most provide only soft sounds. Most slates require two hands to use.

Locator Calls

Locator calls are designed to make turkeys gobble but not approach. Simulating gobblers, predators, or pest species, these calls come in a wide range of designs. The gobble tube is a bellows-operated diaphragm call. These are mainly limited to making the gobble and are widely used for locating roosting gobblers in the spring.

Mouth-blown predator, owl, and crow calls are also used as

Photo by Mike Strandlund

Locator calls, simulating the sound of a crow, owl, hawk, gobbler, or other animal, are used to prompt toms into gobbling and giving away their location. Some of the best "owlers" simply use their voice.

turkey locator calls. Some experts can make very realistic owl calls with their voices; others use elk bugles that produce a loud, squawky whistle. Actually, just about any sudden, loud noise may elicit a gobble.

Which Call to Use

Beginning turkey hunters are often at a loss when considering which call to use. Be aware that anyone can learn to call turkeys into camera or gun range. The degree of success depends on the seriousness of your effort, the time you spend practicing, and the quality and amount of your calling instruction. Ideally, get some advice and practice with borrowed calls until you get an idea of what you want. When practicing, concentrate on the rhythm and intonation of the calls. Pitch makes little difference; there are turkeys with low voices and turkeys with high voices.

For novices, the pushbutton, grooved, or box call should be first choice. The box call may give a truer sound, but will require more practice than the pushbutton or grooved call. Quality box calls are a lifetime investment, and they have been responsible for more successful turkey hunts than any other type of call.

They can produce a yelp, cluck, purr, cackle, and gobble when skillfully operated.

A good second choice for the beginner is the slate call. Although not as loud as the box call, it produces some of the most authentic clucks, yelps, and purrs of the wild turkey.

Before purchasing a friction-type call, test it if possible. Every turkey hunter has an idea of what a call should sound like, and no two calls produce exactly the same sound.

Serious hunters go afield with at least two calls of different types. Often a hunt's success depends on a caller's ability to produce a variety of clucks and yelps using more than one type of call. A gobbler may not respond to a mouth diaphragm but literally run the caller down responding to a box or slate call. The opposite situation is also true: A bird that fails to respond to a box or slate may come running to a diaphragm. A bird may even refuse to respond to a certain pushbutton call while eagerly responding to another of identical design. Each call has its own sound and not even experts know exactly which call will draw a response from a bird.

Learning to Call Turkeys

When and where to use certain types of calls is discussed in the hunting chapters. Remember to use your calls with discretion. Some birds respond to a lot of calling, but don't overdo it. Poor callers often complain, "The turkey hung up and no matter what I tried, he wouldn't come any closer." Most likely, it was all that "trying" that made him stop in the first place.

By the same token, don't be afraid to experiment. When one thing doesn't work, try something else. Develop a calling instinct. Learn from both your successes and failures.

Getting good with a new call requires experimentation. Practice regularly and follow instructions. Tips from an experienced caller can help greatly and condense learning time. Another helpful aid is an instructional tape or record. These explain proper procedure and give helpful tips. Actual videotaped turkey hunts and live recordings can demonstrate real turkey sounds and answer many questions. Memorize turkey sounds by listening to live turkeys. Domestic and wild turkeys make the same basic calls. Tape record yourself making calls, and compare that tape to a calling instructional tape.

The ultimate mastery of turkey calling is learning to imitate turkey talk with your voice. Just about anyone can learn to do it with enough study and practice.

Photo by Mike Strandlund

Studying tapes and books, along with lots of practice, will help you learn how to call turkeys. If you can, get personal instruction from an expert or attend a turkey hunting seminar.

Contests

Friendly competition among turkey hunting buddies has evolved into organized calling contests nationwide. Calling while turkey hunting is much less tedious and certainly more fun than competitive calling. Unlike contest judges, turkeys are not so critical and allow occasional goofs without writing the caller off. All turkey calling takes time and practice, but successful competitive calling demands the ultimate in skill and finesse. Judges of competitive calling are notoriously strict. Contestants joke that a live turkey would probably lose because of calling errors.

A guideline for most calling contests is to put as much as

possible into each call, and express it as an individual bird in a particular situation. If asked for a yelp, give it some excitement, or perhaps a tone of security, aggravation or even alarm. When a lost call is requested, the rendition should contain an expression of alarm in the pathetic cry of a young bird seeking the comfort of other turkeys.

Remember, a good caller must be patient and disciplined. As either a hunter or competitive caller, master each call—be able to call very loud, very soft, and everything in between. Constant practice and experimentation are essential.

Chapter 3
Guns, Bows, and Turkeys

Photo by Earl Hower

To take a trophy tom, a hunter must fully understand his gun, loads, and shooting limitations. Your choice of gun or bow depends on the hunting situation and personal preference.

The moment of truth had arrived, and he knew the gobbler was his.

It had been 30 electrifying minutes of thrilling maneuvers and a ringing *gobble-obble-obble!* answering each series of subtle scrapes the young man made on his slate. Now the hardbreathing hunter, head down and shotgun poised on his knee, was ready when the strutting tom's bright head finally appeared over a rise 40 yards away. The bead settled, the trigger tripped, and a booming report shattered the tension-filled air.

The excited young man jumped to his feet and charged toward the small knoll, eager to get his hands on his first trophy bird. But when he reached the crest, there was nothing. Nothing but a far-off sound of crashing undergrowth, telling a cruel tale of an escaping turkey. The hunter was heartbroken.

That's a sad story of how one man discovered the importance of getting to know his gun and load before taking them hunting. The sad part is he could have gotten his gobbler with just a little preliminary practice. Sadder still is that this story is repeated many times each season.

Knowing Your Gun or Bow

Most big game hunters realize the importance of zeroing their rifles and practicing at various yardages. Waterfowlers usually spend time at a trap and skeet range to hone their wingshooting skills. Both study ballistics, ranges, and load effectiveness before they go hunting.

But it seems that many turkey hunters, especially beginners, do not spend the time they should getting to know their guns and loads. Perhaps they are preoccupied with learning to call; maybe they think all shotguns throw a straight charge and can't believe they could miss a still target with a shotgun. But many of these hunters learn the hard way how mistaken they are. Good accuracy, tight pellet patterns, and knowing your effective range are critical for success at the climax of the hunt.

Choosing Turkey Guns and Bows

Your decision to use a shotgun, rifle, handgun, blackpowder gun, or archery gear largely depends on your hunting methods, shooting interests, and the laws of your state. The vast majority of turkey hunters are shotgunners who get the most satisfaction from calling a bird to close range, or occasionally flushing and wingshooting. Rifles and handguns are legal in some areas and are especially popular in the West; marksmen find turkeys are elusive long-range targets. More hunters today are using muz-

Photo by Mike Strandlund

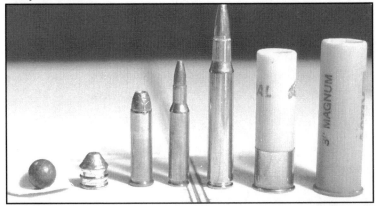

The loads you use must match your hunting technique, shooting range, and safety practices.

zleloading rifles or shotguns to increase the challenge and rekindle the ways of the American frontier. Some turkey hunters use bow and arrows for the ultimate test of their woodsmanship, stealth, and shooting skills.

There are many opinions concerning turkey hunting arms, but there are a few constants. The turkey is a hardy animal for its size, tough to kill unless shots are well placed within effective range. Heavy wings, bones, muscles, and body feathers protect vital body zones from shotgun pellets. Most vulnerable is the head/neck area, but the brain and spinal cord are also protected by bone.

Shotgunners usually use a 12-gauge with high-speed or magnum loads of medium-size pellets. They shoot for the head at around 40 yards maximum, depending on their load, pattern, and shooting skill. Range should be closer and loads should be heavier when body shots are necessary.

The best rifle and cartridges or bow and arrows is the combination that produces best accuracy and sufficient energy without overkill.

With a rifle or archery gear, a turkey must be hit in the head, neck, spine, or heart and lung region or he'll have a good chance of escaping, perhaps to die later. A misdirected shot that strikes the legs or breast ruins a lot of meat. The only way to prevent this is to test and practice with your equipment, learn its limitations, develop your skill, and get to the downed bird as quickly as possible.

47

Photo by Mike Strandlund

By far, most turkeys are taken with shotguns and loads designed for close-range head shots on standing birds.

Turkey Shotguns and Loads

Most turkey hunters believe that calling a wary bird into shotgun range is the essence of turkey hunting and the surest way to make a clean kill.

The most popular turkey guns are full-choked 12-gauge pumps or automatics. The double-barrel shotgun is also a fine turkey gun, steeped in hunting tradition. A 12-gauge with a

48

three-inch chamber or 3½-inch chamber (rather than the standard 2¾-inch) allows use of the longer magnum loads that contain more powder and pellets. This extends shooting range somewhat and is more effective at any range.

The 10-gauge is increasing in popularity among turkey hunters. It offers a few extra yards of range (though not as many as some hunters think) and its heavy pellet charge provides a denser or bigger close-range pattern for surer kills. A consistent-patterning 10-gauge 3½-inch magnum, in the hands of a hunter experienced with it, may be the ultimate turkey gun—provided the user can carry it all day.

The 16-gauge and the three-inch 20-gauge magnum have proportionately less range and effectiveness, though some of the smaller-gauge magnums are better than some lighter 12-gauge loads. Anything less has dubious killing power and should not be used for turkey.

Which Type of Shotgun?

There are several considerations in choosing a shotgun. Autoloaders and pump actions each have their own advantages and disadvantages. A pump (slide) action requires a shooter to consciously chamber a second shell after firing the first, while an autoloader (semi-auto) does not. Occasionally a turkey hunter

Photo by Mike Strandlund

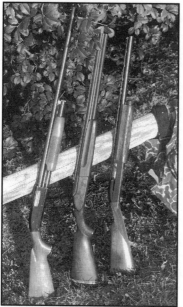

The most popular shotgun types among turkey hunters include the pump or slide action; double-barrel (shown in over/under design); and the semi-auto or autoloader.

needs an autoloader's extra split-second of speed in getting off a follow-up shot. The recoil absorption of a semi-auto can also be an advantage in allowing smaller persons to shoot bigger loads comfortably. But autoloaders are generally more expensive, hardder to maintain, and more likely than other actions to malfunction in adverse conditions. They also tend to be the heaviest—a factor that becomes increasingly important for every ridge you climb.

Double-barrel shotguns are preferred by many turkey hunters. They offer a quick follow-up shot—but only one. There are many double-barrel shooters who wished they had a third shot as they watched a turkey escape within shooting range. Some double shotguns shoot a little differently from each barrel; with tight patterns, this could be the difference between a hit and a miss. A few shooters believe guns with side-by-side tubes are a bit more difficult to point and carry. But the double's reliability and choice of chokes make it the favorite of many turkey hunters.

Chokes and Barrels

In most situations, a tight pellet pattern is desirable for shots at standing turkeys. This ensures you get maximum range from your shotgun and loads and that more pellets reach the intended target within that range. Some hunters place such importance on a tight pattern that they have their barrels customized for the densest shot swarm possible.

These modifications may involve constricting the muzzle to an extra-full choke, perhaps with an insert, or it may even involve honing the choke wider. Some guns, when shooting larger pellets, actually shoot a tighter pattern through a more open choke. Larger pellets compressed in a tight choke may jam together, deform, and fly erratically as they leave the muzzle.

A double-barrel shotgun provides the advantage of two chokes in the combination you think is best. A full/modified combination of chokes enables a hunter to send a dense pattern of smaller pellets at the turkey's head and follow with a larger pattern of larger pellets to penetrate the body. This may be desirable if the first compact charge of shot does not connect and the turkey begins an escape; a wider pattern with the second shot may make a hit more likely.

Now that more shotgunners realize longer barrels offer little in extra velocity or pattern density, more turkey hunters are going for shorter barrels around 21-24 inches long. A shorter barrel makes a gun a little lighter and easier to handle while walking in rough terrain. It is also quicker to point and less likely to bump against an obstruction as it is moved into shooting position. And it gives the turkey a little less to see.

A shorter barrel has a shorter sighting plane, however, which reduces pointing precision. A tube-top rib aids the turkey shooter, who must aim his tight-patterning shotgun as he would aim a rifle. An extra sighting bead at mid barrel allows the hunter to line up the two beads as he would align a front and rear sight. A few dedicated turkey hunters actually do install open sights, low-power scopes, or electronic sights on their shotguns. Best equipped with a large center-dot reticle, these scopes are a clear advantage in low-light situations. But they may be a disadvantage in a fleeting opportunity.

Photo by Mike Strandlund

Some turkey shotgunners use iron sights, scopes, or electronic sights for precise placement of their pattern.

Turkey hunters often equip their shotguns with slings, especially when they have to tote a big 12 or 13 pound 10-gauge in rugged terrain. A sling should have quick-detachable swivels so you can take it off when you set up to call. Shotguns should also have a non-glare surface in the form of temporary or permanent paint, tape, or custom finish.

Shotgun Loads

There is considerable difference of opinion on shotgun ammo for turkey hunting. But there's no argument that the wild turkey is hard to bring down, and that hunters have a responsibility to use loads powerful enough for quick kills.

Suitable turkey loads have a powder charge of at least 3¾ drams equivalent (heavier powder charges are preferred) and propel at least 1⅜ ounces of No. 2, 4, 5, or 6 shot. A few hunters shoot No. 7½ or BB, but these should be used only under special circumstances.

There are three approaches to shotgunning turkeys which have evolved three contradictory theories on selecting shotshell loads for the big birds.

Photo Courtesy New Mexico Game and Fish Department

The wild turkey is a hardy animal with small, shielded vital zones. Scattergun shots must be well placed from close range.

The first philosophy recognizes that a standing turkey's feathers and bones protect him too well for routine body shots, and the vital area presents a very small target. The turkey must be called to short range and shot in the head and neck with a dense, high-pellet-count pattern to ensure multiple hits, this theory states.

Another view is that turkeys are often difficult to coax within 40 yards, and only larger pellets retain the energy needed to take big birds at maximum ranges where they often "hang up," or stop approaching. Past 40 yards, No. 7½ and some No. 6 shot loads slow and spread so much that they are no longer lethal to a turkey.

The hunting methods and ethics of a few hunters result in running and flying body shots, and most of these hunters believe in only the heaviest loads of the largest pellets—nothing smaller than three-inch magnum loads of No. 2.

Each of these approaches is legitimate under the right conditions, but each has flaws. A dense pattern of shot such as 6s or

Photo by Earl Hower

The surest way of taking a turkey with a shotgun is to use heavy charges of medium-size pellets, shooting for the head at under 40 yards. Try body shots only in special circumstances.

53

even 7½s *is* the most deadly at short range, perhaps 25 yards or less. But smaller shot lacks the ability to penetrate skull and neck bones at longer ranges. It is admirably sportsmanlike to wait until a bird has approached within 25 yards before taking a shot. But a gobbler turning to leave at 35 yards is a temptation too great for most hunters to resist, and at that range, the7½s might only make him leave quicker.

No. 2 and 4 pellets hit hard enough to penetrate bone up to 50 yards or even more, depending on shot size, hardness, and velocity. But the sparceness of such a pattern at that range makes it ineffective. An ounce and a half of 2s hold only one-fourth as many pellets as an equal measure of 7½ shot, which makes for a much smaller or thinner pattern. Since at least a couple hits are necessary in a turkey's head and neck zone, which is only the size of a large spoon, it is easy to miss with the longer shots.

Hunters who take body shots on turkeys use the largest pellet sizes, up to BB where legal. They run the risk of failing to center the moving target in the pattern, and of making a split-second decision that causes them to shoot at an out-of-range bird. There is also danger of the big pellets going astray and reaching an unintentional target. If a hunter uses a tight pattern on moving birds, he runs greater risk of missing. If he uses a wider choke, pellets that connect may be few and far between; these hunters inadvertently depend on lucky head or neck hits—a very poor practice.

The Best Turkey Loads

What's the best compromise? Most experts agree that No. 5 shot or one size either way, in the tightest, hardest-hitting load available, is the way to go. No. 4, 5, or 6 shot offers a sufficient pellet count and good downrange pellet energy. The heavier pellet charges, up to two ounces in the three-inch 12-gauge and 2½ ounces in the 10-gauge, provide the extra pellets that increase the chance of multiple hits. Each extra quarter ounce of lead gives you about 34 more No. 4 pellets, 42 more No. 5 pellets, and 56 more No. 6 pellets.

Simply adding more pellets does not necessarily increase the effectiveness of your load, however. Many 12-gauges throw better patterns with 1½ ounces than with 1⅞ ounces. There may be significant differences between 1⅜-and 1⅝-ounce patterns, or the patterns of similar loads made by different companies.

A given powder charge shoots a heavier lead load at a lower velocity. Since velocity is just as important as pellet mass in determining penetration, this is a major consideration. A velocity difference of 100 feet per second or so is not that critical, since the difference in velocity diminishes downrange. But if the difference is much greater, it can reduce penetration significantly and shorten your effective range.

You can get this velocity back by using higher powder charges with magnum or light-magnum loads. The resulting higher velocity, when accompanied with other load improvements, can extend your range by about 10 yards over standard loads.

These improvements include plastic buffering and harder pellets, which decrease the pellet deformation that destroys patterns. Lead pellets containing larger amounts of antimony, or hardener, resist deformation better than softer lead pellets coated with copper or nickel.

Another development is the duplex shotshell load with both large and medium-sized pellets. The theory is that the large pellets retain maximum energy while the smaller pellets make the pattern denser. This concept has gotten good reviews, but it neither has the pattern density of medium-pellet charges nor as good a chance of making multiple high-energy hits as a large-pellet load.

Some hunters believe they maximize their shooting effectiveness by first loading their gun with a shotshell that has a smaller pellet size for close-range pattern density, followed with shotshells of increasingly larger pellet size—supposedly for better retained pellet energy as a turkey makes its escape.

This idea is fine as long as the shooter is not firing at long range, just hoping for a hit from a single heavy pellet. He must only shoot within range of his pattern, and to do this, he must *know* the range of his pattern.

Patterning Your Shotgun and Loads

Different shotgun loads, even two brands with identical specifications, can give amazingly different performance. The deciding factor of a load is not the data that's printed on the box; it's the pattern the load prints on target paper. Test-firing at paper targets shows whether your gun is shooting where you point, and whether it shoots a good pellet formation. It helps you find the best combination of gun and load, determine your range, and build confidence in your shooting.

Use a patterning sheet for the most scientific information on pattern accuracy and density. Draw a bullseye in the center of a large piece of paper at least 40 inches square. Hang or tack the paper vertically in a safe shooting area. Assuming a steady

It is essential for shotgunners to pattern their guns and loads before taking them turkey hunting. Determine your maximum effective range, and stick to it.

position, such as sitting or on a bench rest, hold the shotgun's bead at the bottom of the bullseye and fire.

Take the patterning sheet down, determine the center of the densest part of the pattern, and mark it. Compare this mark to the bullseye to determine the accuracy of the shot—the pattern shouldn't be more than three or four inches off center.

Draw a 30-inch circle around the center mark, using a template or large compass. (Make the compass by driving a nail into one end of a wood strip, then drilling a quarter-inch hole 15 inches from the nail. Tack the nail into the center of the pattern, hold a pencil in the drilled hole, and draw a circle by pivoting the wood strip around the nail.)

To find the percentage of pellets that struck within the circle, count your hits within the circle, multiply this total by 100, and divide that figure by the average number of pellets in each load.

(Yes, you have to cut open some shells and count the shot.) For example, an average 1½-ounce No. 4 load holds 203 pellets; if you had 165 hits in the 30-inch circle, the equation is 165x100 = 16,500 divided by 203 = .81, or 81 percent.

You can go one step further and divide the pattern into quadrants to determine if there are consistently more pellets in one area of the pattern. A good pattern has a fairly equal distribution of pellet holes throughout the 30-inch circle. For most purposes, turkey hunters strive for the most pellet holes possible in the 30-inch circle, reflecting the desirability of tight pellet groups.

The number of hits and percentage of hits are figures used for comparing the patterns of different loads. For an accurate comparison, at least five shots from every load should be averaged. For easy future reference, write information about the gun, load, range, and pellet counts on the patterning sheets.

Life-size Targets

To get an idea of how the pattern would actually strike a turkey, use a life-size turkey target such as the target sold by the National Rifle Association. The NRA target also has a predrawn 30-inch circle to compare aim/impact points and to make pellet counts.

Illustrations Courtesy Missouri Department of Conservation

Patterning your shotgun on a life-size target will tell you the density and point of impact of your pattern at various yardages. Diagram A shows a good pattern for the larger pellet sizes—well centered on the head with over a half-dozen hits in the head/neck area. Pattern B is too sparse; C is too low, a crippling shot, while D is too high and so tight it would be hard to place accurately.

The turkey target shows the accuracy of your pattern. Tight patterns do not allow much room for poor accuracy. If your gun doesn't shoot where you point, you may have to adjust your aim, do some gunsmithing, or replace the barrel or shotgun altogether. The worst situation is when a shotgun shoots low, which easily cripples but doesn't kill turkeys.

The target also indicates how many pellets on the average strike the turkey's vitals from a given load at a given yardage. Use this information to determine which loads give the best consistency and to learn your favorite load's range limitations.

Determining Load Performance

What kind of performance is necessary from a shotgun load to bring down a turkey? Where does the line fall between shoot and don't shoot? All-encompassing answers to these questions do not exist because there are so many variables involved. But there are some general guidelines, the foremost being: If you're not sure, try for a better shot.

The main dilemma deals with pattern and range, specifically the number of pellets that must strike vital organs for a sure kill. As a general rule, heavier loads of No. 2 shot should place at least four pellets for every shot into the head and neck area. No. 4, to be effective, should connect with a minimum of six or eight pellets, and No. 6 should consistently send home a full dozen. These figures are minimums, not averages; if you find that an occasional shot can't make these standards, try another load or shorten your range.

To determine your best load, select three or four likely loads and begin patterning one at 10 yards. This short-range test will show if your gun can accurately place softball-size patterns. Aim at the center of the neck, so that a well-placed 12-inch pattern would cover the head and base of the neck. At longer ranges your pattern will cover an area considerably larger than the turkey itself, but the long distance can cause you to miss. Aiming at the center of the neck helps you concentrate on an accurate shot.

Using the same load, increase your range by five yards for each group of shots, recording your results at each yardage. When you reach the point where your pattern becomes too sparce, you've gone beyond the maximum range for that load. Go through the same process with at least a couple other loads, and hunt with the one that gives the best results.

Pattern testing can be more interesting and fun if you do it

VITAL AREAS

Bony skull and vertebrae (Penetration will immobilize)

NON–VITAL AREAS

A Esophagus or gullet
B Trachea or windpipe
C Wattles
D Snood or dewbill
E Loose neck skin

This diagram, drawn with the aid of an X-ray, shows the anatomy of a turkey head in actual size. Only pellet penetration in the shaded area will immediately down a turkey. Hits elsewhere may be fatal, but the hunter may have difficulty recovering the bird. You may make photocopies of this page for a life size turkey head target.

(Art by John Idstrom, From X-rays by Dr. Paul H. Pelham, DVM., Courtesy Minnesota Dept. of Natural Resources.)

with a shooting club or a few hunting friends. You can help each other with problems or questions you may have, and a little friendly competition may lead to discovery of the best combination of gun and load for the best results.

Turkey Shotgunning Techniques

While patterning your shotgun, practice your shots as they would be in a hunting situation. Try to duplicate actual field conditions, wear complete hunting gear, and work on estimating yardage with life-size targets. Practice shooting with both eyes open.

Photo by Earl Hower

Practice shooting while sitting on the ground in full turkey hunting gear—including headnet. Your clothing and position can affect shooting ability.

Develop a consistent shotgun shooting form based on the way you would actually shoot a turkey. This usually starts with a sitting position, knees upraised, and the gun or your arms rested on your knees or the inside of your thighs. Shoot from other positions, too. Learn the best hold and sight picture for centering the pattern on your aiming point, and practice with that method for all your shooting. If you plan to wear a headnet while hunting, practice shooting in different positions with your headnet in place. You may find your mask obscures your vision at certain angles, and it may need adjustment or replacement.

Turkey Rifles and Loads

Most turkeys bagged with rifles are taken by hunters pursuing both turkeys and deer. Some specialist marksmen hunt only turkeys or turkeys and small game or varmints at the same time. The category where you fit determines the gun and load you use.

Probably the ideal turkey/deer factory load is the .243 or 6 mm,

NRA Staff Photo

Rifles are legal for turkey hunting in some areas and preferred by some shooters. Good accuracy and load selection are needed to hit turkeys without crippling or destroying meat.

though the .30 calibers are popular. Hunters who aren't concerned with bringing down a deer lean toward the .22-caliber centerfires, the .22 magnum, and perhaps the .17 caliber.

Though single-shots and bolt-action rifles are generally the most accurate, any action type will do. The important thing is knowing the accuracy limitations of both you and your rifle.

The problem in selecting a rifle caliber for turkeys is finding the best compromise with sufficient energy to anchor the game without causing extensive meat damage. Turkeys have been known to escape even though hit midbody with a .30-06 bullet. On the other hand, a shot in the breast with even the smallest centerfires may make the turkey unsalvageable.

In conquering this dilemma, the way you shoot a turkey with a rifle is more important than the rifle you shoot him with.

Shooting Turkeys with Rifles

Shot placement is critical in the fine line between a quick kill and meat destruction. A bullet in the head or neck is obviously best, but in most cases shooting at that tiny, constantly moving target is out of the question. The best shot is at the base of the neck or high at midbody, just high enough to keep from striking the breast, preferably at the junction of the shoulder bones and spine. These areas are roughly twice the size of the head/neck, are not as prone to movement, and a shot here will kill instantly. Conversely, a shot that strikes the legs, breast, or abdomen may be fatal only after the wounded bird eludes the hunter.

Aside from good shooting skill and an accurate gun/load combination, a solid rest and a scope of 1½x to 12x or variable, depending on your hunting style, will do the most for good shot placement. A good high-power, high-resolution scope lets you shoot at longer ranges (up to about 150 yards for good marksmen) and under lower light conditions. There are problems with scopes, however, such as trying to find a close bird in a high-power scope, and trying to find anything in a scope that has become wet or fogged.

Riflemen who hunt turkeys must exercise extreme caution for several reasons. Errant bullets travel much farther than shotgun pellets and are more dangerous to humans once they get there. A poorly placed shot on a turkey can ruin both the trophy and food value of the bird.

The best spot for shotgun pellet placement is No. 1. The wing butt/spinal cord, indicated by No. 2, is the best location for bullet or arrow placement. No. 3 is a crippling shot, while No. 4 would destroy the breast meat.

Selecting a Turkey Rifle and Load

While a responsible rifleman takes only shots that are not likely to damage meat, some slight deviation is inevitable. There are loads available that minimize meat damage while still retaining good accuracy.

The .22 magnum rimfire should be considered the minimum rifle load for turkeys. Within 100 yards, the body weight/energy ratio makes the .22 magnum on a turkey the equivalent of a .243 on a large whitetail buck.

The .22-caliber centerfires, including the .222, .223, .22-250, .220 Swift, etc., are the most popular among long-range turkey hunters. They have high velocity necessary for the accuracy that flat-shooting bullets provide. They have ample energy to kill a turkey, but they also have ample energy to destroy meat with a low, forward shot.

The .22 Hornet is an exception. Its lower velocity leads to less bullet expansion and less tissue damage. Rifles and ammo for this older caliber may be difficult to find, however.

There are other ways to lessen the effects of bullet expansion. Some turkey hunters use the high-velocity loads with full-metal-jacket bullets. The problem here is that the bullet passes through the game so cleanly that it imparts comparatively little shock and the turkey often escapes.

A better approach is to download ammo so that it has a lower velocity and less shock and bullet expansion. For example, a .22-250 cartridge with a muzzle velocity of around 3,000 feet per second can be handloaded with less or different gunpowder to a velocity of about 2,000 fps. It is still accurate at this velocity, but will not blow up on impact and destroy meat. This works even better with the .30-caliber cartridges, though downloading has a greater effect on the trajectory of heavier bullets. Lighter loads can be purchased for common calibers such as the .30-06 if you do not reload your own.

This is the route many deer/turkey hunters take. As long as their cartridges are well marked, they can safely hunt both deer and turkey with one gun and ammo perfect for both—perhaps a .30-06 with full loads for deer and downloads for turkey. This can lead to problems of having the wrong cartridge chambered in a certain shooting situation, however.

Other options for clean kills with minimal meat damage include bigger-bore rifles with solid, nonexpanding bullets, and the older, slower, hard-nosed loads in the medium calibers, which expand little. These include the .30 Carbine, some .30-30 and .32 Specials, and similar loads. These may represent overkill, but not to the degree of the .270 or .30-06.

In any of these cases, the hunter should not sacrifice bullet placement for a less-damaging load. A high-energy bullet in the lower neck will cause less destruction than a slower bullet in the breast. Like the shotgunner, the rifleman should test various loads at various ranges until he learns the limitations of his gun, ammo, and shooting ability. The rifleman should determine his best accuracy by shooting from a bench rest and sandbags, then *practice* shooting in full hunting gear and in realistic game-shooting positions.

Photo by Mike Strandlund

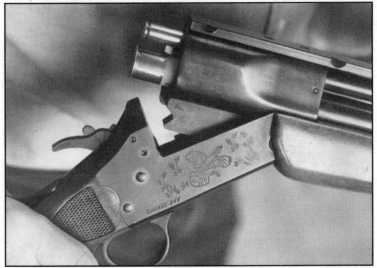

A combination rifle/shotgun such as this Savage Model 24 gives a hunter the choice of a shotgun for close-called birds or a rifle for longer-range work. This gun is chambered for 20-gauge Magnum and .222 Rem.

Rifle/Shotgun Combinations

Some turkey hunters believe the ideal firearm is a combination rifle/shotgun such as those made by Savage, Ithaca, Valmet, and various European gunmakers. These guns offer the short-range sureness of a shotgun with the longer-range capability of a rifle, but there are drawbacks. Each barrel is a single shot, and few of these combo firearms offer a 12-gauge barrel (most are .410, 20, or 16 gauge). Since the barrels are very difficult to align perfectly, the shotgun tube may pattern off-center after the rifle barrel is zeroed.

Muzzleloaders and Turkeys

One way to enhance the romance of turkey hunting is by using the guns of your forefathers: a muzzleloading rifle or shotgun. But before you start, remember that turkeys today are smarter than the ones hunted with the original smokepoles, and most hunters today aren't quite as keen in their woodsmanship skills as those old buckskinners who practiced them daily. In other words, be prepared for a real challenge if you step into the turkey woods with a muzzleloader.

Photo by Mike Strandlund

More hunters today are using muzzleloading rifles and shotguns to increase the challenge of turkey hunting and to explore the ways of pioneer hunters. With blackpowder arms, load development is critical for accuracy and sure kills.

Muzzleloading hunters have many options to choose from. In ignition systems, the percussion cap is more reliable and easier to shoot. Others find the flintlock more aesthetic and traditional. They may choose a rifle, which experienced black powder shooters can use for turkeys to 60 yards or so. Or they may choose a big-bore shotgun, which could reach about 35 yards with a good load.

Best rifle calibers for accuracy and energy on turkeys are .36, .40 and .45. However, a .50 caliber you can shoot more accurately than a .45 is better, of course.

Muzzleloading shotguns are less efficient than their smokeless counterparts, so you must make amends. Best is a 10-gauge with up to five drams of black powder and two ounces of shot. Limit your shooting to the range your pattern testing indicates.

The subject of loads for muzzleloaders is a science in itself. It takes a lot of experimenting with different components and careful range testing to come up with the optimum load. Start with a couple good blackpowder shooting manuals and make sure when you enter the woods you have the best possible system.

Bows and Arrows for Turkeys

Hunting a wild turkey gobbler with bow and arrows ranks among the ultimate tests for hunting and shooting skill. The bowhunter must get very close to a turkey, then draw and release undetected,

Photo by Michael Hanback

Bowhunting an elusive gobbler ranks among the toughest challenges an archer may face. Thorough practice is essential.

then hit a small vital zone only a few square inches in size.

A heavy bow is not necessary to penetrate a turkey, but more pull means less arrow trajectory and usually better accuracy. The greater velocity a heavier bow provides also decreases the chance a turkey will "jump the string," or move out of the way between your release and the arrow's arrival.

The type of bow and shooting method you use are a matter of personal preference. Most bowhunters today use compound bows and sight pins, but a practiced recurve or longbow shooter aiming instinctively can approach or exceed the accuracy of a high-tech archer in many hunting situations. The bare-bow archer can shoot faster, but the compound shooter can hold full draw longer.

Always use broadheads when hunting turkeys—three or four blades are better than two, giving you the extra inch or so of cutting area that may reach an artery or vital organ. A helpful item is the Judo point—a spring that fits over the arrow shaft just behind the broadhead. The spring uses friction to keep the arrow from passing completely through the turkey. With the arrow still in its body, a wounded turkey will get hung up in brush and be less able to escape. The Judo point will also help prevent lost arrows, as will flu-flu fletching. Flu-flu arrows use increased air resistance to make arrows drop after a fairly normal

Photo by Mike Strandlund

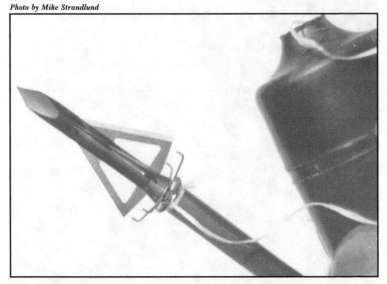

Bowhunters should use the same broadheads for turkeys as they do for deer. A Judo and tracking string may help prevent lost arrows and lost game.

flight of about 35 yards. They may affect accuracy and restrict range, however.

The vast majority of turkey bowhunters use calls, due to the short ranges necessary. Because of the movement involved in drawing the string, many turkey bowhunters build a blind to hide their drawing motion from an incoming turkey. Full camouflage in clothing and equipment is mandatory, especially on glossy-finished bows. A folding stool keeps bowhunters in a good position for drawing the bow, and a decoy helps distract a gobbler from the motion.

Handguns for Turkeys

Like muzzleloading guns and archery gear, handguns are gaining popularity among hunters seeking more challenge in their sport. In the few states where they are legal, handguns have helped turkey hunters find a new, exciting approach to going after gobblers.

Because handguns have limited accuracy and turkeys are small, often long-range targets, the more accurate, scoped, single-shot pistols are a favorite. With a scope and experienced hand, guns like the Remington XP-100 (a bolt-action single-shot) and the Thompson/Center Contender (a hinge-action) can be very effective for turkeys. The accuracy of these pistols approaches that

NRA Staff Photo

Handguns, especially scoped, single-shot pistols, can be effective for taking turkeys in the hands of marksmen.

of rifles, and the guns are chambered for a variety of loads from .22 to .44.

A good handgunner with an open-sighted revolver or auto-loader can legitimately shoot turkeys out to 40 yards or so. The slower velocity and lower energy of solid-point loads in .38 Special, .45 ACP, .357 Magnum, and .44 Magnum minimize meat damage if shots are well placed.

One giant step further into the realm of supreme hunting challenge is the blackpowder revolver. Legends tell of Confederate soldiers, stripped of their long guns following the Civil War, who survived by hunting with their percussion revolvers. If you are so inclined, avoid the .36-caliber revolvers, which shoot balls with energy only about equal to a .22 Long Rifle bullet. Consider only the .44 or .45 calibers, work hard on load development, and *practice*.

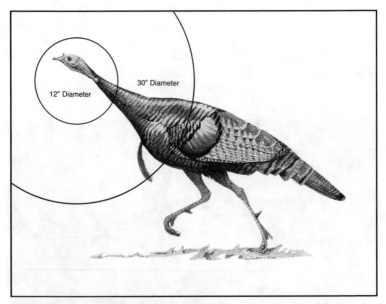

Life-size turkey targets, such as this NRA version, are valuable practice aids no matter what type of gun or bow you use to hunt turkeys.

CHAPTER 4

GEARING UP FOR GOBBLERS

Gearing up for turkey hunting is, in many respects, the most critical part of the hunt. Some hunters learn this the hard way when they can't get a gobbler close because they've chosen the wrong call, or spook the bird because of poor use of camouflage. Hunters who wound and lose a turkey because of the wrong gun or load pay a high price for their negligence.

It's important in more ways than one to have the right stuff when it comes to turkey hunting. The equipment needed on a turkey hunt falls into four categories:

- **Clothing and Footwear**
- **Calling and Decoying Equipment**
- **Miscellaneous Hunting and Woodsmanship Gear**
- **Guns and Ammo or Bows and Arrows**

Photo by Mike Strandlund

Besides guns and calls, a turkey hunter needs good clothing and useful accessories to make hunting more enjoyable and productive.

Hunting Clothes and Footwear

The first priority in selecting turkey hunting clothes is that they be camouflaged or at least a drab color that will blend with surroundings. More and more, turkey hunters are putting emphasis on complete camouflage specially adapted to the habitat. You need to conceal movement, shape, and color in that order of importance. With the right camo, you can look like the forest floor, a bush, or an extension of a tree base.

More important than selecting the *best* clothing for turkey hunting is making sure you don't wear the *worst*. Clothing that is red, white, blue, or shiny black may attract the attention of another turkey hunter and, since those are the colors of a spring gobbler, could happen.

Some turkey hunters have been successful while using blaze orange to alert other hunters to their presence. An increasingly popular technique is tying a strip of orange material around the tree where the hunter sits. There's considerable evidence that this is a handicap to bagging a bird, but it does improve safety.

Camouflage

While you may choose to use some blaze orange, it is important to conceal your body from the turkey. Vegetation, season, and weather conditions all play a part in the type of camouflage color, pattern, and fabric that's best. It is a mistake to believe all camouflage is the same. Some camo clothes are too light-colored. Some are too dark, while others have too small a pattern or not enough contrast and appear to be solid-colored at a distance. Buy camo clothing made for hunters, not "fashion" camouflaged clothing.

In most cases where your camouflage is critical, you will be sitting against a large tree in relatively open woods. It is important that you blend with your background, whether the turkey is looking at you head-on, with the tree as background, or from the side, with the open woods as background.

In the mountains or northern hardwoods, most turkey seasons open in spring and close in fall with little green vegetation present. Brown leaves, bare brush, and tree trunks are the predominant features in this place and time, and should be reflected in your choice of camouflage. Brown leaf patterns work fine in many cases, and since it can get cold this time of year, many hunters use the same clothes as late-season waterfowl hunters. The brown pattern blends well with a background of dead leaves.

In early fall or late spring, when the forest is green, the hunter

Photo by Mike Strandlund

Camouflage clothing should match the surroundings as closely as possible. This hunter, planning to hunt while sitting against a tree, has pants in a woodland pattern to blend with fallen leaves and shirt and cap to match the tree bark. He is attaching cloth "leaves" to velcro strips on his shirt for a very effective three-dimensional effect.

should dress accordingly. Green woodland patterns blend well with a background of pines or broadleaf bushes.

Certain all-season or interchangeable patterns are increasingly popular with knowledgeable hunters. Patterns that simulate tree bark are very effective, blending amazingly well with the trees and fairly well with most general backgrounds. Some hunters combine types, such as a tree bark jacket and brown camo pants, to blend the best with backgrounds of bark and dead leaves.

Another newer type of camouflage consists of a drab garment with velcro fasteners at various locations. To these fasteners are attached fake cloth leaves with different patterns and colors. This type of camouflage can be matched to either green or brown background, and the three-dimensional effect it gives is incomparable camouflage. One drawback is that if the hunter stirs, the movement may be accentuated in the "leaves" clinging to his clothes, and that movement is more dangerous to betraying your position than color or pattern.

Camo Accessories

Camouflage should be from head to toe. The entire face should be covered; in fact, this often-neglected detail is probably the

Photo by Mike Strandlund

A well-camouflaged hat, headnet, and gloves are important clothing accessories for the turkey hunter. They cover light-colored skin and help hide movement.

most important aspect of camouflage. The face is the most visible part of your body and the most frightening to any game animal. A headnet should have see-through mesh or eyeholes small enough that your face is fully covered, but large enough to permit clear vision even when you turn your head. Or, you can wear camo makeup in black, green, and brown. Make sure everything is covered, including ear lobes and eyelids. If you wear glasses, make sure they are also covered and cannot flash in the sun. Glasses will flash right through the mesh of a full-face headnet sometimes. The shade of a big-brimmed hat is the best prevention for this.

Hands are the second most important to conceal because of their movement and light color. Lightweight camo or dark-colored gloves are ideal, though you can use grease paint here, also. Make sure gloves don't interfere with your ability to shoot. Some hunters cut off a glove's trigger finger.

Boots should also be dark-colored or camo, or you may conceal them under a pile of leaves or behind a log. If you do, make sure it doesn't restrict your movement or make movements more detectable by an incoming turkey. Remember, the soles may be exposed when you are sitting. They should be dark; if they're light, keep them out of sight.

Clothing Considerations

Make a final check of your camouflage in front of a mirror, sitting in your calling position. Look for things like white socks visible between your cuffs and boots; a bright T-shirt sticking out at your neck; parts of your face or hands uncovered; a bright shirt suddenly exposed when you raise your gun; shiny buttons, zippers, tags, or wristwatch. Your gun or bow should be camouflaged with tape or paint.

Since most turkey hunting is during transitional seasons, a variety of weather conditions can occur and you should be prepared. April or November can range from shirtsleeve conditions to driving snow in many areas.

If you're going on a several-day turkey hunting trip and could encounter a variety of weather conditions, it's best to bring a wardrobe of camo gear including T-shirt, heavier shirt, jacket, and raingear to ensure your outerwear will always be camouflaged.

If you wear the T-shirt in very warm weather, put camo makeup on your arms. If it's colder, a waterfowler-type parka is good, but make sure it isn't noisy when you move or so bulky that it restricts you from raising your gun. Raingear should also

Good camouflage raingear can save the hunt when clouds burst. Avoid cheap vinyl suits; they are noisy and short-lived.

be as quiet as possible, have a dull finish. Vinyl raingear is short-lived and shiny when it's wet; rubber-backed cloth is better.

Besides camouflage and protection, hunting clothes must have other qualities. They should be durable. Tough clothing not only protects you from the briars; it resists wear. Cheap clothing may fade quickly with washing and become too light to be effective camouflage. Broken fasteners or ripped pockets can be a considerable problem in some situations. In the long run, high-quality clothing performs better and is usually more economical than one-hunt apparel, and it makes hunting more enjoyable.

Clothes should be functional. Practical turkey hunting pants and jackets have several large pockets to carry calls, shells, lunch, and other field gear. A hood protects you from the cold, wind, and rain, and helps camouflage your head and neck (but may hamper your hearing). Since much of a turkey hunter's time is spent sitting on the ground, waterproof pants with insulation in the rear have saved many from misery.

One of the most useful clothing accessories is the specialized turkey vest. Depending on the manufacturer, it offers camouflage, a snap-out padded seat, backtag holder, several roomy pockets, and a large game bag. It keeps all your gear together so you can just strap it on, grab a gun, and go turkey hunting.

Footwear must be adapted to the conditions, also. Leather boots should be waterproofed with oil, wax, or silicone. During cold spells, an insulated boot is usually best, while hunters who cross rivers or hunt areas like the big swamps of the Southeast are better off with quick-drying, camouflaged tennis shoes or hip boots. A good compromise is the knee-high rubber boot with a deep-track sole, along with socks selected according to weather

Photo by Mike Strandlund

A very functional item is a turkey hunting vest. In a variety of designs, they offer many large pockets for stowing gear. Some have built-in seat pads and game bags.

Turkey hunting boots should be suited to terrain and weather. It helps if they are camouflaged, and it's imperative they don't have shiny hardware or conspicuous soles.

Hats are important; style is a matter of personal preference. Requirements are that they be camouflaged, brimmed, and suited to the elements. The baseball-cap and Jones styles are most popular. A couple of companies make a style with a built-in headnet, a very functional and convenient design.

Calls and Decoys

The pivotal piece of equipment a turkey hunter carries is the call. Nearly everyone who pursues turkeys today uses calls designed to make the turkey come hunting the hunter. Knowing which to use and how to use it is a prime ingredient to succcess.

The most popular calls today depict a hen turkey's wide range of vocalizations. The wooden, plastic, slate, and rubber devices accomplish this with friction or vibration. (This is covered in more detail in the "Turkey Calls and Calling" chapter.)

You'll choose your turkey calls after finding which ones produce the best sound for you. It's generally a good idea to carry and be proficient with at least a couple of different calls. A certain gobbler may not respond to a near-perfect putt on your diaphragm call, but come galloping to the same call on a slate.

You'll also want locator calls that sound like an owl, crow, hawk, or gobbler. These calls surprise, frighten, or anger a bird into gobbling and giving away his location.

Most calls are rather fragile, so be careful not to break them or get a slate or box call wet. A box call must be secured with a rubber band, or you should place a piece of cloth between the lid and box, to keep it from squeaking.

Some hunters use decoys in hunting, and while they aren't a substitute for good calling, they are a good supplement. They may also serve as a range marker. Because they help give you a standing shot where you want it, they help prevent a crippling loss. Before you buy a decoy, however, make sure they are legal where you plan to hunt. Remember to use extreme caution in using a decoy, because they can draw fire from irresponsible

Photo by Mike Strandlund

A turkey decoy is very effective in persuading a spring gobbler to come those last few steps. Decoys are rather inconvenient to use, however, and can be hazardous in some situations.

hunters. Decoys should not resemble gobblers in any way and should not be used in the fall.

Commercial turkey decoys are in full-body or silhouette shapes, each of which have advantages and disadvantages. Full bodies are usually more realistic, but are more difficult to carry. A strap or hook attached to the decoy helps, but a bag is better. It covers the decoy and reduces the possibility of a hunter mistaking you for game. A blaze-orange bag enhances this safety factor.

Other Gear

Carrying the right pieces of equipment, knowing how to use them, and leaving unnecessary gear at home can increase your probability of success and enjoyment, and make you more comfortable while turkey hunting. Make a list and update it periodically so you're always in the right gear. Here's a sample list:

A **pad** to sit on can protect you from the cold, wet, hard ground. Most turkey hunters do so much sitting that a pad is well worth carrying. There are several pads on the market, or you can make your own from burlap and styrofoam pellets or other such material. The pad should be camouflaged and firm. A strap serves as a carrying aid.

A **portable blind** is used by some hunters. This may be as simple as a large piece of camouflage cloth. It helps hide lower-body movements when calling a turkey in close.

Topographical maps and a **compass** are often used by seasoned turkey hunters to find likely hotspots, decide strategy, and plan stalks on gobbling birds. They not only help you return to camp with a bird, but help you return to camp, period. If you spend a lot of time hunting in unfamiliar country without these little items, plan on losing time and spending time lost.

Topo maps show the woods and fields, ridges and draws that tell an experienced hunter where the birds are likely to be (more on this in the scouting chapter). To order maps, contact: Branch of Distribution, U.S. Geological Survey, Box 25286, Denver, CO 80225, Tel. (303) 236-7477. Maps shipping and handling may include a nominal fee. Indexes to identify the maps you need may be ordered free of charge.

If you don't already have a compass, buy a good model, either pocket or pin-on. If it's pin-on, take it off in a calling situation. Learn how to use your compass, and use it when finding your way into and out of difficult woods.

Unless you're hunting a real wilderness area where survival measures may be necessary, a **small knife** is best for its lightness

Photo by Mike Strandlund

With a topo map, compass, and notes taken during scouting, a hunter may plan strategy for the most likely way of taking a turkey.

and likely applications. Whether it is a pocket or sheath knife makes no difference. A Swiss Army knife is helpful in some situations, especially if your hunting trip involves several days of camping. Some campers find the large survival knife with a serrated back edge to be useful.

To get on even terms with a turkey's awesome eyesight, many hunters carry a compact pair of **binoculars**. They can be a great aid in glassing a distant field for birds or to identify an indistinct object.

A filled **canteen or thermos** and a snack will keep you going through a long day of hunting. The food and drink should be compact as possible and not easily perishable. If you know there is plenty of potable water in the area you hunt, you may bring along a small cup in lieu of the canteen, and save a few ounces of baggage.

In some areas during some seasons, one of the most vital items in your kit might be **insect repellent**. Swatting at gnats or mosquitoes will invariably ruin your chances of calling a gobbler to the gun; enduring the stinging and biting makes for a miserable hunting experience.

Because turkey hunters commonly carry so much gear, the method of carry becomes important. You may need a **fanny**

Photo by Mike Strandlund

Binoculars are valuable to locate turkeys, identify their sex, observe them from a distance, and get a closer look at anything in the woods.

pack, or prefer a **backpack.** Carrying a camera or binoculars is much easier with a **Yukon Harness**, which hugs the unit close to the body, keeping it from swinging but making it easily accessible.

Don't forget your **huning license, back tag, stamps, and written permission** if you're hunting on an area where they are required.

Depending on the type of hunt you're on, assorted tools and camping gear will make it smoother and more enjoyable. Here's a list of other things you might need:

- **Flashlight or Lantern**
- **Prescription Medications**
- **Rope**
- **Camera and Film**
- **Axe, Saw, or Machete**
- **Extra Footwear and Clothing**
- **Cooler**
- **Tent, Stakes, and Stake Driver**
- **Fire-Starting Materials**
- **Waterproof Tarp**
- **Shave Kit, Wash Rag, Towel**
- **Food and Drink**
- **Toilet Paper**
- **Camp Stove**
- **First Aid, Snake Bite Kits**
- **Heater**
- **Extra Batteries and Fuel**
- **Cooking and Eating Utensils**
- **Sleeping Bag, Pad, and Pillow**

CHAPTER 5
SCOUTING AND HUNT PREPARATION

The turkey hunter who just "goes hunting" without thorough preparation is cheating himself. The less a hunter plans or practices, the more he has to depend on luck. His odds for bagging a gobbler take a nosedive. And even

Photo Courtesy of Robby Rohm

The best turkey hunters realize their goal by being well organized and doing their homework.

if the hunt is successful by chance, it lacks the fulfillment that comes with diligent effort and executing a plan. When you've done your homework, paid your dues, and hunted hard, you have satisfaction knowing that the results of skill—not dumb luck—is what weighs heavy in your game bag.

Setting up a turkey hunt involves scouting, anticipating situations, and minding the small details that will increase your chance of success. The amount of preseason work you have to do depends on your turkey hunting experience and familiarity with the hunting area.

The many elements of preparation include the following:

- **Physical Conditioning**
- **Practicing with Calls**
- **Knowing Guns and Loads**
- **Preparing other Gear**
- **Studying Turkeys and Tactics**
- **Finding Hunting Areas**
- **Locating and Patterning Birds**
- **Planning Strategy and Logistics**
- **Miscellaneous Planning**
- **Lining up a Guide (if applicable)**

Physical Conditioning

While your style of turkey hunting may not be physically demanding, reasonable physical conditioning is important. Sometimes it can make the differance between success and failure; if you are not fatigued, you can hunt longer, cover more territory, and be more alert. Too, strength and endurance may be the most important things of all in case of an emergency far from help.

The best conditioning for any physical activity is doing lots of that activity, along with aerobic exercises such as jogging or bicycling to increase your stamina. If you hunt in the mountains, hike the hills with a hefty backpack and do knee bends with weight on your shoulders to build leg muscles. If your work is not strenuous enough to keep you in shape, establish a routine of jogging and weight lifting or doing floor exercises like situps and pushups. Routine exercise year-round is better than a crash program just before hunting season.

It's a good idea to do some of your running and walking exercises in the boots you plan to wear hunting, so you and your hunting footwear get used to each other.

Photo by Mike Strandlund

The amount of planning and preparation put into a turkey hunt often determines its success. Start planning well before season and continuously update your knowledge and strategy.

Practicing with Calls

How good do you have to be with a turkey call for a reasonable hope of success? That's a question up for debate. But one thing is for sure: The better you are, the better your chances.

The only way to get good with a turkey call is to obtain expert instruction, then practice, experiment, and practice some more.

Buy your turkey calls well ahead of season and practice in your spare time. Many hunters carry calls with them and practice at any opportunity—such as while driving, waiting, or working out. Study instructional tapes and seek advice from experts. Dedicated callers audition for the real experts—gobblers themselves—prior to hunting season. If you go this route, however, you're well-advised to not mess with turkeys you plan to hunt, or they'll get an education in turkey hunting, too.

Knowing Guns and Loads

The importance of patterning shotguns, zeroing rifles, and practicing with bows and arrows cannot be overemphasized. Before hunting, be sure you've tested all the components you will use on your hunt. Shoot the loads you'll use in the gun you'll use in the clothes you'll wear. Make certain of the range and capabilities of your gun or bow, and realize the limitations of your skill.

Preparing Other Gear

The importance of complete familiarization with your gun or bow and calls is explained in those chapters. You must get acquainted with other gear also. Break in new boots well before hunting time. Repair or replace things like old tents, faded camouflage clothing, leaky raingear, or worn footwear. If you buy new equipment like a tent, turkey decoy, or turkey vest, learn how they operate so you can use them in the dark. Anticipate the small, easy-to-forget things that make a trip easier or more enjoyable; some duct tape, a plastic bag, or a roll of toilet paper seem like minor items, but they can make a major difference. Test your camp stove, heater, or lantern to make sure they work, and check your fuel can for leaks. Get your things organized early and thoroughly so you have everything you need and don't waste hunting time.

Studying Turkeys and Tactics

Before you scout for turkeys and a place to hunt, take advantage of the knowledge acquired by biologists and hunters before you. Study books and magazine articles, videos and audio tapes on turkey hunting. They can give you quick insight into the behavior of turkeys and different perspectives on how to hunt them. When you step into the woods you should know just what to look for and what it means.

Photo by Mike Strandlund

Hunters who spend time living with turkeys learn the most about them. A comfortable camp in turkey country puts you in a good position to study birds.

Finding Hunting Areas

Job one in pursuit of a turkey is finding a good hunting site. If you're new to turkey hunting or new to an area, you've got to start by looking at the big picture, locating general areas of turkey habitation. Then gradually narrow it down to a certain area, then a certain piece of property, then specific hunting sites.

Game biologists, sporting goods dealers, hunting club members, and others in the know are a good place to start. They may be able to put you onto a good site, but more likely they'll give you a county or part of a county to check. Harvest records may give you some clue to an area's turkey population, but don't depend on those figures entirely.

You may also consult *Guide to the American Wild Turkey*, published by the National Wild Turkey Federation. It shows the range and concentration of wild turkeys in each state and is updated on a regular basis.

The best turkey hunting land is available to hunters who spend time talking to locals and exercising good landowner relations. Always get permission before hunting private land.

With a place in mind, make sure you have proper permission to hunt. You may need a permit or special stamp if it is public land, and you'll need permission (maybe written) if it is private.

Get topographic maps of the area, and use them to identify places with hunting potential. In the East and Midwest, it may be large wooded areas with steep ridges, which provide turkeys with safety through cover and inaccessibility. In the West it may be wooded canyons in bare mountains, or near scarce water sources. In the South, cypress swamps may be the preferred habitat.

Topo maps will also give you other valuable information, indicating logging roads and hiking trails that allow deep woods access, or powerline and gasline corridors that attract birds and carry the sound of your owl call—and the gobbler's response—a long distance. A topo map, compass, and skill in using them can help you pinpoint and reach a gobbling tom's location.

Make as many trips to the area as you can well before the start of the season. If you are hunting close to home, you have the advantage of being able to keep a check on the area for several weeks prior to the opener.

Locating and Patterning Birds

The key to turkey hunting success is getting close to birds. This requires finding toms or flocks of turkeys, monitoring their behavior, and attempting to pattern their movements so you have a good idea where they will be at given times. Spring scouting is particularly productive, since breeding flocks won't travel far from the center of their territory under normal circumstances.

Photo by Mike Strandlund

Spring gobblers are most easily located by covering a lot of ground at dawn and dusk, eliciting gobbles by sounding a locator call.

Spring Scouting

In spring, the favorite way of locating toms is to travel through known turkey habitat and pinpoint locations where you hear gobbles. You may simply walk the woods when turkeys gobble most (around dawn or dusk) and listen for gobblers sounding off. Or you may entice or challenge them into gobbling with a locator call. Walking trails or driving back roads, stop every couple hundred yards and sound a crow, owl, hawk, or predator call, or maybe a gobble tube. At each spot you stop, call toward different directions and try different calls. Being territorial, turkeys challenge many other animals that invade their turf. Sometimes, toms are so "hot" they will respond to almost any audible stimulation, including train whistles and slamming car doors. Other times, especially during harsh weather, gobblers are reluctant to answer. Slight variations in your locator call may make the difference in getting them to respond.

Some hunters use loud turkey hen yelps to locate gobblers, but this method can backfire. A tom could sneak in unannounced and take you by surprise. If he does, you can bet he'll be much harder to call when hunting season rolls around. If you're scouting after dusk and you're sure turkeys are on their roost, you don't have to worry about gobblers coming. But if they see you walk away or hear your car, they may become suspicious of your particular call. You're better off with one of the non-turkey locator calls.

Cover as much ground as possible during the first and last hour of daylight. Call in areas where sound will carry far. Concentrate on distant toms—those close to the road are easily heard and usually draw the attention of several hunters. Remember that the lay of the land will influence the sound of a gobble. If both you and the turkey are on a powerline corridor, he will sound closer than he actually is. If he is behind a ridge and late spring foilage, he will sound farther away.

Experienced hunters can sometimes tell the difference between an immature tom and a trophy by the sound of the gobble. A weak, broken gobble, equivalent to the voice of a teenage boy, is a jake or subordinate tom. The gobble of a mature, dominant bird is high- pitched with a clear, confident ring.

Listen hard for far-off gobbles; a distant tom may be able to hear your call and sound off just within hearing range. Use landmarks to pinpoint gobbling sites. Make special note of locations where you hear gobbles several different days. Check the area at midday, trying to locate favorite roosting trees. If you find some, make note of an easy, sure method of approaching close in the dark.

Patterning Spring Birds

Turkeys are not always found where they were last fall and winter. However, gobblers are often found where other gobblers were found the previous spring. The reason is simple. Gobblers seek hens; hens seek good nesting areas. Good nesting areas are used year after year.

Photo by Mike Strandlund

Check dusty and muddy areas for dusting sites and tracks. You may be able to determine travel patterns of turkey flocks and figure out how to intercept them.

When scouting, try to learn where the gobbler roosts, whether he has a harem, and where the hens lead him. Since there's no hunting pressure, he will probably gobble frequently, and following him should be easy.

If you can, shadow the gobbler. Try determining where he goes and when. Try to find his strutting ground, his center of activity. This area is usually a partial clearing or very open woods close to good roosting trees. Turkeys spend much time loafing, displaying, and breeding in their primary strutting grounds.

Gobblers strut in early morning and are often heard and seen in meadow or field corners before the season. A spotting scope may help you quickly search wide areas of pastures and fields. A hunter can learn where gobblers have been sighted by talking with truckers, mailmen, farmers, and school bus drivers—people who travel the roads during the early hours—and people who talk with early-morning travelers, such as waitresses and gas station attendants. Locating a half-dozen gobblers will greatly enhance your chances of scoring.

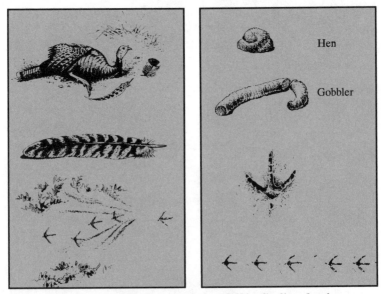

You can locate turkey flocks in spring or fall by finding dusting areas, droppings, scratchings, or tracks. Dusting areas (above left) are depressions in dry, sandy soil—sometimes on anthills. Look for dropped feathers nearby. Scratchings are areas where turkeys scrape to the bare ground looking for food. J-shaped gobbler droppings can be distinguished from roundish hen droppings (above right). Look for turkey tracks in mud and soft, bare earth such as cultivated fields.

Fall Scouting

While springtime scouting is locating gobbles more than anything else, fall turkey hunting is more reading the landscape, searching for sign, looking for places you'd *expect* turkeys to be and then seeing if they *have* been there.

Start by checking areas with good fall foods. Acorns are the turkey's staple fall and winter food in many areas, but you may find patches of more desirable food with turkeys concentrating there. Wild grapes are a favorite, as are farm crops and various

Photo by Mike Strandlund

In fall, check for scratchings in forests of oak or other nut-bearing trees. Turkeys leave obvious sign as flocks forage for food, scratching through fallen leaves to the bare ground.

wild seeds and berries. Turkeys will frequent fields and clearings where there are large fall hatches of high-protein insects.

The best way to locate a fall flock is to find scratchings—large areas where birds have pawed the leaves searching for acorns or other food. As a turkey scratches for food, it claws the leaves back and to the side, making a V that points the way the bird was heading. If you have a hard time distinguishing the V, remember that there will be a pile of leaves at the backside of the scratch. If the scratchings are very recent, you should be able to follow them to the flock.

Other sign to look for includes dusting areas—depressions about two feet in diameter filled with dust that turkeys regularly visit. These are often found along old roads, field edges, and ridge tops. Also look for the large droppings of turkeys. The roundish droppings are left by hens, while the long, J-shaped ones are made by gobblers.

If it's dry, check out watering places. A scarcity of water will cause turkeys to pattern their movements to bring them by a spring, pond, or creek a couple of times daily. Search the muddy perimeters of streams, ponds, and puddles for turkey tracks.

Photo by Mike Strandlund

Where turkeys come onto pastures and fields, you can often pattern their movements with a spotting scope. Window mounts are very convenient for spotting from a vehicle.

With experience, you may be able to tell the thicker-toed tracks of a mature gobbler apart from those left by hens and young birds. The hunter should do preseason scouting to locate these high-traffic turkey areas and decide where the turkeys are most likely to be. Make notes and maps of areas where you find good turkey food and signs of turkey activity. After two or three seasons of studying an area, you may be able to intercept turkeys quite easily.

Fall turkeys can also be located by finding their roosting sites. Get in a likely spot and listen for birds flying to and from roosts early and late. Toms occasionally give away their location by gobbling in the fall. Keeping in touch with people in the area can often result in a tip on the location of a flock.

Planning Strategy

Once you feel you have the turkeys nailed down, it's time for one of the most fascinating phases of turkey hunting: planning strategy.

Most hunting strategy is a Plan B or Plan C, made during the day's hunt after Plan A has failed. But Plan A, made prior to the season or often the evening before the hunt, is often a hunter's best chance.

Planning strategy, you use your best knowledge of where a particular bird will be or where he will go. Combine that with your knowledge of tactics and calling, information about the terrain, and turkey hunter's intuition to take your best shot at coming up with a trick to fool old tom.

Some strategies are old standbys: Roost a bird, then sneak in close as you can well before light next morning. Locate a bird just before dawn and approach to calling distance. Pattern a gobbler's line of travel, then work around and let him come to you. Get between the areas where a flock roosts, feeds, loafs, or waters. Flush a fall flock, hide where they were, and try to call them back. Set up an ambush where a flock comes onto a field or mountain meadow.

Whichever plan you use, you must customize the strategy to meet the special circumstances. Take advantage of a grassy logging road for a quiet roost ambush. Set up at a strutting area if the gobbler won't respond from his roost. Team up with a buddy to trick a wily old bird. Bring a dog and/or portable blind for fall hunting.

Turkeys are cagey game animals that can make the best-laid strategy look silly. You have to use all your resources: Knowledge of area, the game, and tactics; topographical maps and a compass; stealth and woodsmanship; skill with call, camo, and gun.

Photo by Mike Strandlund

A topo map, compass, and knowledge of the area are important tools to help you plan turkey hunting strategy.

Miscellaneous Planning

Putting all you have into the hunt means paying attention to all details and anticipating problems you might encounter.

It might seem like a minor detail, but having to arise at 4 a.m.

is a considerable factor in turkey hunting success. A tired, bleary-eyed hunter is operating with only a fraction of his physical and mental ability. *Practice* waking up early so it doesn't come as a shock on opening morning. And, by the way, can you depend on your alarm clock to get you up then?

Here are some other details to consider: Plan your hunting time well in advance so you don't have to cancel because of work or other obligations. Make sure your vehicle is in good shape and won't leave you stranded. Make sure you know the way (in the dark) to your hunting site. Buy your licenses and stamps before they're sold out. Drink nothing stronger than cola the night before hunting, and go to bed early. While hunting, mentally rehearse turkey encounters so you are mentally prepared, avoid overexcitement, and don't make a mistake when a bird appears.

Hiring a Guide

Turkey hunters that are inexperienced or unfamiliar with their hunting area sometimes hire a hunting guide. A good guide can greatly increase your odds for success and provide a valuable education in turkey hunting.

Reliable references are the best way to decide on a hunting guide. If you don't know anyone who can recommend a guide where you want to hunt, get a list of area guides, contact them, and request a list of references. You can obtain the addresses of guides through advertisements in newspapers and magazines, and through local chambers of commerce. Start looking at least a year ahead of time and book several months before the season.

Your early contacts will give you an idea of a guide's professionalism and concern for your needs. Use references to make a final decision on the guide to hire.

Once you've selected a guide, make sure you both know what your obligations will be: when and where you will meet, where you will hunt, how long you will hunt, who is responsible for transportation, and other such details. If you outline your plans and responsibilities through correspondence, it can serve as a simple contract.

Success is not the result of award-winning calling, gold medal shooting, or the hunting instincts of Daniel Boone. It is the dedication to success that makes you get fit, learn and practice all you can, go to bed early, spend every possible minute in the woods, and try your hardest when you're there. That moment the gobbler steps clear of the laurel, so close his colors dazzle you and his brazen gobble seems to ring the mountainside, you'll be glad you did your homework.

Part II

How To Hunt
The Wild Turkey

Photo by Charlie Farmer

CHAPTER 6
SPRING GOBBLER HUNTING

Spring gobbler hunting is a tactical game of using a turkey's bold courtship behavior against him. The fascinating part of this game is that the bird's general conduct is fairly predictable, but his acute senses and inherent wariness make him an elusive target. Gobbling, a temperamental tom "calls" an

Photo by Mike Strandlund

Few outdoor experiences equal the thrill and challenge of calling a spring gobbler to the gun.

eager hunter close, then disappears like a wisp of morning mountain mist. Legions of turkey men who begin the season bright-eyed and basically sane end it with red eyes and talks with themselves. Only about 5 percent will bag their bird, but they'll all be back next year. It's all part of the game.

A hunter after gobblers in spring uses an intimate knowledge of turkey habits, woodsmanship, stealth, and calling. Superior skill in one area can make up for lack of experience or expertise in another. But consistently successful turkey hunters invariably have honed their skills in all areas.

There are five steps in hunting spring gobblers:

- **Finding Gobblers**
- **Setting Up**
- **Calling Strategy**
- **Spring Hunting Tactics**
- **Making the Shot**

Finding Gobblers

Remember that finding gobblers in spring involves more listening than looking. Gobblers sound off frequently as they establish their pecking order through fighting and dominance displays. All the mature male turkeys in an area try to establish a breeding territory. Usually the territory is a certain piece of real estate with indefinite borders. In large northern hardwoods, breeding gobblers may have a "mobile territory" that moves as the flock moves. As the birds attempt to move in and out of overlapping territories, toms fight and gobble at each other until an order of dominance is established and each area has a boss gobbler. The pecking order and the gobbling are important to the hunter.

Roosting a Gobbler

If the wild turkey gobbler has a weakness, it is his habit of gobbling from his roost—announcing to the countryside exactly where he plans to spend the night and where he'll be at daybreak. By far the best way to increase your odds of success is to put a gobbler to bed—pinpointing his roosting tree in evening—and getting there silently and unseen before first light next morning.

Roosting habits vary somewhat among the subspecies. Because big trees are scarce in the arid Southwest, roosts are limited and Rio Grande turkeys are fairly easy to bid good-night. Eastern birds, living in huge forests of big trees, are at the opposite end of the spectrum. Merriam's turkeys, especially those in arid areas, prefer to roost in pine trees within gliding distance to water.

Photo by Leonard Lee Rue III   Photo by Michael Hanback

Your best chance of calling a bird at first light is to locate a tom by getting him to gobble from his roost, then get as close as you can without spooking him.

Florida turkeys roost mostly in cypress trees or flooded timber over shallow water, which offers protection against night-stalking predators.

Turkeys often roost in trees or groups of trees that stand out among others as larger or with heavier horizontal branches. Because survival depends on unpredictability, they seldom spend consecutive nights in the same roost, though they will use good roosts regularly and year after year.

You can sometimes locate highly favored roosting sites by the accumulations of droppings and feathers on the ground below. But the easiest way to locate roosts, and to find where birds are sleeping on a particular night, is by hooting or otherwise causing a gobbler to scold at dawn or dusk.

Make the bird gobble, then close the distance fast without getting too close. Stop, make him gobble, then get closer, until you can pinpoint his tree or group of trees. If it's morning, look for a spot to set up. In the evening, you'll have to mentally mark the spot and return in the morning. When the roost could be difficult to find again before dawn, you may mark the way with pieces of light-colored tape or tissue.

Most hunters roost gobblers at dusk, with plans on returning next morning. This is the safest approach in areas where only morning hunting is allowed. Causing a tom to gobble in the foredawn invites competing hunters and a possibly dangerous situation.

Though toms don't gobble as much in evening, roosting at dusk is also more effective. You can make a mistake and even

105

disturb a gobbler slightly at dusk without it ruining the morning's hunt. Blow it in the morning and you'll have a very suspicious, uncooperative bird to work.

Setting Up

The outcome of many turkey hunts depends on the hunter's ability to get in an optimum position to call a gobbler. The idea is to pick your way as close to the gobbler as possible, so your initial calls sound like a hen in easy reach, without tipping him off to your true identity. You improve your chances of calling him in with each yard you advance. But the odds of spooking him and completely blowing your chances increase with each step you take. There is often very little margin for error here.

If you're approaching a gobbler in daylight, be careful to avoid openings. He may spot you and spook from over a quarter mile away.

Though each situation is different, 150 yards is generally a good distance to set up from a bird you roosted or heard gobbling. Much depends on the lay of the land, the surrounding underbrush, and moistness of the ground. When the woods are dry and open, don't push your luck and try to get too close, or

Photo Courtesy Missouri Department of Conservation

A gobbler will be more cooperative if you set up in an open woods without any fences, streams, or other obstructions between you and the bird. Sit against a large tree for concealment and safety.

a gobbler will pinpoint you with his eyes and ears. Remember, a turkey can see you in the moonlight and hear noises you may not even know you are making. Attempting to get too close is among the most common causes of ruined turkey hunts.

In some cases, conditions are ideal for sneaking in close. If it is fairly brushy, foggy, or there is an obstacle to hide your approach, and if the woods offer quiet walking or there is wind or rain to cover your noises, you might be able to stalk within 50 yards. Utilize a creek or dry streambed, deer trail, road, or anything you can to mask the sound of your approach. When you can't walk silently, you may try to sound like a stutter-stepping deer or rustling squirrel, rather than a man with his rhythmic *crunch, crunch, crunch....* The best hunters, in rare situations, can actually slip in close enough to scare off hens but not the gobbler, thereby eliminating the competition for their calling!

Set-Up Alternatives

Sometimes the situation is just not right for setting up close to the tree. You may not be able to get there unseen, or there may even be another hunter there already. In that case, your best chance may be to set up at the strutting area or the fly-down spot. Strive to position yourself in the area where logic or actual knowledge tells you the bird will probably land. Granted, this is very difficult to determine. But the beauty of this strategy is that even if your calling is mediocre or the gobbler is wise to hunters, he may land in your lap without any need for your calling.

Scouting has hopefully shown where a gobbler wants to go or where he has traveled before with his hens. Good turkey hunters know these probable travel patterns and set up along the route. Hunters who find the gobbler going the other direction may have set up in an area the turkeys intentionally wanted to avoid.

Positioning

Taking a position, avoid getting on the other side of streams, fences, deep gullies, and thick brushlines. Turkeys depend on intelligence and eyesight for survival, and when their eyesight is hindered, their intelligence tells them beware.

A good set-up site is in a "clean woods," a forest with lots of good-size trees and a minimum of thick litter or brush at ground level. Gobblers are less leery if they can see well. Also, you can wait until a turkey's head is behind a large tree so your final move into shooting position is undetected.

If the predawn sky is clear, consider the relative positions of the turkey and the rising sun. You may have a hard time spotting, identifying, or shooting a gobbler between you and a low sun. The gobbler may be hesitant to approach or circle behind you if he must walk into a blinding sunrise. Sit in a position where the sun does not handicap either you or the bird.

Wary gobblers know that if danger strikes, it is much more difficult for them to escape if they have to go uphill. For this reason, they prefer to approach a caller by walking on level ground or an uphill slope. Never set up below a gobbler. If there is any type of trail nearby, set up there and watch for the toms to walk down the path—they often do.

Photo by Mike Strandlund

Position yourself on the same level or uphill of a gobbler. Pull your knees in close and point your gun in the direction of the bird as you begin calling.

Set up against a large tree, stump, or ledge that will hide your outline. Don't hide behind something—try to blend into the surroundings. Turkeys know that predators hide behind things. But they're not smart enough to think that when they see nothing, a hunter could be part of that nothing.

Make sure no trees or brush impede your vision or your gun swing. Rake away any noisy leaves and twigs from your calling site. Get comfortable, because it might be a long wait, and a comfortable hunter moves less than an uncomfortable hunter. Seat pads, such as those built into turkey hunting vests, will help keep you still.

Position yourself with your feet pulled in close and your knees upraised. Allow the gun to rest on a knee with the buttstock in tight to the shoulder. In this ready position, you can go from calling to shooting with a minimum of movement. If you are right-handed, set up with your left shoulder pointed toward the bird's probable direction of approach. This way you can swing the gun on a wide arc and accurately point over a wide area.

Once you're in position, keep absolutely still while working the gobbler. Hunters who can't keep still usually never see their bird before it spots them and departs. If you're using a call that requires hand motion, hide the movement from the bird. Even if the turkey is a long ways off, hold still to keep from frightening squirrels or small birds, whose actions will betray your presence.

Calling Strategy

Spring calling strategy is dependent on the particular bird, hunter, and situation. Calling techniques vary considerably, even among experts. Here are some recognized practices and tips.

Always make sure there is enough light (and it's legal shooting time) before making your first calls. If you call too early, the gobbler could fly down right after your first series of calls while it is too dark to shoot. He could detect you or lose interest before there was enough light. On the other hand, don't wait too long, or the gobbler might fly off the roost to a hen.

With the gobbler still in the tree, begin calling with mild clucks or a few soft yelps. Don't call too often or too loudly; this is unnatural for roosting birds and will make the gobbler suspicious. It also increases the chance of making a bad note that identifies you as a fake. Calls should be so soft a man could not hear them 50 yards away (a turkey will have no trouble hearing them from over 100). If you get an immediate gobble in response, stop calling and get ready. You're in one of the best possible positions to kill a turkey.

Occasionally a gobbler will come running to the call, but you won't see it much among dominant birds. These turkeys usually get killed or wised up the first time they are hunted. Be ready, just in case, with your gun pointed in the direction of the gobble.

If you get no response, wait several minutes after good light to see if the gobbler makes a move. Have patience. Then you may call very sparingly. The tom may answer you a few times, then gobble sporadically or go silent. The gobbler's vocal reaction to your calling doesn't necessarily reveal his intentions. A hot-gobbling tom may be working himself into a frenzy to come looking for you. Or he may be determined to call to him the hen he thinks he hears. A silent gobbler may be preparing for the right moment to come looking for you, or he may be tipped off to your presence; he may be gone, or he may be on his way toward you. The best situation is when the tom gobbles regularly so you can monitor his movements. If he's silent, watch your flank in case he circles behind.

As the minutes pass, or if the gobbler flies down, hunter's intuition comes into play. If you think the bird is interested, remain silent or call sparingly. If he's not convinced, you may need a new approach. You can try a fly-down cackle on a box call or diaphragm, along with loud leg-slapping to simulate the sound of wings. A variation in calls, such as whining, purring, and clucking may convince him to come your way. Once he's in view, you must use a diaphragm or other call that does not require movement, or you must remain quiet.

Photo by Mike Strandlund

If a gobbler ignores your tree yelps, you may get his attention by cackling and slapping your leg with your cap to simulate the sounds of a hen turkey flying from her roost.

When you hear a gobbler fly down, remain in position without calling; he may be on his way over. Even if he seemed to fly in the other direction, he may have done so only because there was a place there where landing was easier. If he doesn't appear presently, give a few calls to regain his attention. If that gets no response, and you didn't hear him leave, wait 20 to 30 minutes

Photo by Leonard Lee Rue III

Keep track of a tom by the sound of his gobbles. Don't respond to every gobble with a hen call; if you seem too eager, the gobbler may hold his ground, expecting the excited "hen" to come to him.

and call again. No sign of the bird means he is probably spooked or has left with another hen.

The type and volume of your calling should vary according to the circumstances. Again, loud yelping may ruin a good setup on a roosted bird. Calling in general should be discreet. Don't respond immediately to a gobble with a call unless you know you are competing with hens. Constant, loud yelping, a mistake many callers make, is a sure tip-off to a gobbler. It will make him wary or think you're an aggressive hen—the type gobblers expect to come to them. Callers are usually better off with subtle clucks and playing hard to get. (An exception to this is that persistent cutting or cackling can sometimes trip a tom's trigger when nothing else will.)

If you are roaming and calling, set up before calling and start with soft clucks in case you've wandered close to a gobbler. If you get no response and don't believe a tom could be sneaking in, gradually increase volume to get the attention of distant birds. Send the sound in several directions. With no answer still, move about 150 yards and try again. Don't space your set-ups farther

Photo by Leonard Lee Rue III

than that. You may blunder onto a gobbler you could have located by setting up sooner.

Remember too that turkeys are most vocal toward the beginning of spring breeding season, when assertiveness helps establish pecking order. As the season progresses and birds begin to encounter hunters, they generally keep quieter. You should too.

Weather conditions also affect gobbling. Toms are usually quieter in wind, wet, and cold with a falling barometer. Still, clear mornings usually see the most activity. Gobblers are sometimes active at night during a bright full moon, which decreases daytime activity.

Spring Hunting Tactics

A successful turkey hunt consists of convincing calling and excellent positioning. Maneuvering and getting a good position on a gobbler requires strategy and tactics according to the situation. You have to combine knowledge of turkeys in general, awareness of what your particular turkey is up to, ability to plan and execute strategy, and woodsmanship skills. Resourcefulness plays a major role in taking wary toms.

It may take several tries and a variety of tactics, but putting all your skills together will put the gobbler where you want him.

The classic way of killing a gobbler is to call him from the roost or slip in close as he gobbles, then call him the rest of the way. But there are many variations and endless roadblocks the hunter can encounter. Here are a few examples:

- **The gobbler you tried to call off the roost flies down but moves away from you.**
- **A bird comes toward your calling but stops, still gobbling, just out of gun or bow range.**
- **A tom is with hens and refuses to leave.**
- **Gobblers simply won't gobble.**

The first two problems can often be solved with a quick, quiet repositioning. Don't be afraid to move when the gobbler can't see or hear you. If you're on a gobbler, don't let him get away with the hope he may wander back. Remain unseen, but be aggressive. Follow him, pleading with your hen calls. Gobblers do change their minds. Try to plot his course and get in front of him. He may be with a hen that will give him the slip to go lay an egg. When she disappears, the gobbler will immediately look for new company. If you're still there and have not revealed your true identity, he may come looking for you.

When a lone gobbler halts his approach, or "hangs up," it is for one of two reasons: he has encountered an obstruction (as seemingly insignificant as a bush or puddle) or he is skeptical. In either case, wait to see if he keeps coming, walks around, or flies over the roadblock. If not, you may again be successful by putting the move on him. If you think an obstruction is the problem, very carefully move to one side so that he can continue approaching while avoiding the blockade. If he simply seems hesitant, move backward at an angle and call again, simulating a moving hen. His fear of losing a hot hen may overcome his suspicion and keep him coming.

Sometimes you'll find yourself at dawn in the turkey woods, with no bird roosted, and the forest silent of gobbles. You may roam, set up, and call, or you may stay put at a known strutting ground or travel route.

Surmounting problems three and four may require gearing your tactics to match the time of the season. As described in Chapter 1, turkey breeding season progresses through definite stages in which turkey behavior varies considerably. The time when you hunt may coincide with any of these stages. Depending on the phase of the breeding period, turkeys may be more or less vocal, alone or in bigger or smaller flocks, easier or harder to call.

Stages and Strategies

Beginning in March and advancing through May in most areas, the stages of breeding season include turkeys gathered in large flocks prior to breeding, toms recruiting hens, breeding flocks consisting of usually one gobbler and several hens, and lone turkeys (gobblers abandoned and most hens nesting).

Stage 1: Prebreeding Flocks

Before breeding activities begin, turkeys are gathered in large flocks with a mix of gobblers and hens. In these cases, every turkey within thousands of acres may be gathered in a single flock. Locating turkeys at this stage may be very difficult, but when you do, you have hit the jackpot. You may top a ridge to find an immense flock with two dozen gobblers.

Turkeys, both hens and gobblers, are very vocal at this stage. But because there is so much competition with real hens, and toms really aren't interested at this point, gobblers respond very little to calling. They're not yet willing to risk their lives to go looking for a hen. Innovative tactics must be used.

Photo Courtesy New Mexico Game and Fish Department

Very early in spring, turkeys gather in big, mixed flocks with gobblers just starting to strut. Since there are so many real turkeys calling and breeding hasn't begun, toms can be very difficult to call at this stage.

Perhaps the most effective strategy during this period begins with monitoring the flock. Because it is so large, the flock leaves lots of sign and makes lots of noise. You may be able to pattern the flock's movements and find a good point to intercept the turkeys, or you may be able to locate the vocal flock from long distance, figure its direction of movement, and head it off.

There's a chance a gobbler may walk right into shooting range with no need for calling. More likely, you'll have to call. But what if no gobblers respond?

Call the hens. Big turkey flocks take orders from a master or "flock" hen who holds her position through assertiveness—generally vocal assertiveness. There is a definite hierarchy among the hens, and if one hen challenges authority, there is a confrontation. If you vocally challenge the boss hens, they will come to confront you, and the gobblers will follow.

To make this work, you have to play the role of a lone hen that has approached the flock and wants to take over. Yelp and cackle very loudly. Make it coarse, frequent, insistent. If you get a response from the flock hen, make your call louder and bossier than hers. If everything works right, it won't be long before she comes swaggering over to have it out with you—and the rest of the flock comes to watch.

Stage 2: Harem Gathering

The second phase of turkey mating is a time of high activity among gobblers. As their hormone levels increase, gobblers begin

Photo by Leonard Lee Rue III   *Photo by Charlie Farmer*

A frantic time for turkeys, the harem-gathering stage sees toms at peak gobbling, strutting, and fighting activity. If nothing else works, you may try challenging a tom with a gobble call.

establishing territories, fighting each other, and gathering hens into small breeding flocks.

This period, which just precedes the opening of turkey hunting season in most areas, is the easiest time to locate and get close to gobblers. It is the first of two peak gobbling periods during the breeding season. The furious and frustrated toms often gobble all day long with little provocation.

If hunting season hasn't started when this peak arrives, use the time to locate several gobblers. They are establishing territories at this time, and will stay in the same general vicinity.

If this gobbling peak coincides with hunting season, you may encounter three types of gobblers. The first is a gobbler or jake that is subordinate to the harem-keepers. These birds, especially the jakes, are upset with the state of things—their big social group has broken up, maybe they've gotten their tails whipped by a big gobbler, and they're lonely. These birds are the easiest of all to call in most situations, unless they know a bully gobbler is nearby.

You may find a gobbler with a few hens who is looking for some new recruits. These birds may be easy to call, or they may be reluctant to go far from their hard-won harem. You may have to sneak in very close for calls to work. Then there is the gobbler that refuses to leave his hens. The hen-calling tactic described earlier may get results here.

If nothing else works, a last resort is to challenge the gobbler himself. Assume the role of another tom and, approaching as close as you dare, gobble with a gobble tube, box call, or diaphragm. Start by gobbling feebly, sounding like a jake the boss tom would just love to stomp. If this doesn't work, gobble hard like another prime tom. If he gobbles, gobble back. Ideally, the bird feels bold from having just won a few fights, is enjoying the benefits of his battles, and will not hesitate to take on the intruder. Mix in a few hen calls, making him think another gobbler is with a hen in his territory, and you will really make him mad.

Stage 3: Breeding Flocks

When the frenzy of initial courtship and dominance battle subsides, things settle down a bit. Harems are established and have a routine. There are few unspoken-for hens in the woods. Gobblers have no pressing need to announce their availability and sulk, which makes it difficult for hunters.

Non-gobbling toms are hard to locate, but once you do find a breeding flock, there's a good chance you can pattern it. Toms still gobble from the roost, unless encounters with hunters have really silenced them. Since toms almost always roost a few trees away from the hens, a very skillful turkey hunter may be able to sneak between the gobbler and hens before dawn. These are the most effective approaches to hunting during this stage.

If you do locate a flock but the gobbler won't respond to your calls, stay with him. Use a locator call to keep him gobbling and giving away his position. Hens are nesting at this time, laying eggs daily. If you can follow the flock long enough without being detected, you may get lucky and be there at a time when all the hens have gone off to their nests, leaving the gobbler alone. Now is when he'll be vulnerable to a few soft clucks.

Some silent gobblers speak up under certain conditions. An electrical storm may fluster a tom into gobbling, and if you are careful of lightning, this may be a good time to hunt. Nervousness

Photo by Karen Lollo

Shots at this distance are rare. More likely, you'll find your gobbler "hangs up" just out of range, and aggressive tactics may be necessary.

may lower the bird's guard. He may be especially eager for company and the rainfall will make it harder for him to see or hear you.

Often during this phase, as well as in any phase, you'll encounter the gobbler that hangs up just out of shotgun range. It is a common occurrence with various causes—an obstruction in his path, reluctance to go far from a hen, doubts about your calling. You can try waiting him out, or you can try the move-and-call strategy. But these may not work.

At this time you may consider the most aggressive tactic of all—the rush. If the bird is hung up out of sight but a short distance away, you may be able to move toward the bird and get within shooting range before the startled bird takes flight. If you try this technique, be careful not to let it lead you to taking a marginal shot. While the rush may work on rare occasions, it is usually best to come back and try the bird another day.

Stage 4: Deserted Gobblers

When hens have laid their last egg, they abandon the harem to sit on their nests. When all the hens have gone, leaving the gobbler alone, the old boy becomes very distressed. He lets the world know. This is another gobbling peak that usually lasts only a few days.

Photo by Mike Strandlund

If you've been chasing a call-shy gobbler, you may have his movements patterned well enough to ambush him on his travels.

While gobblers are again easy to locate, they are usually very hard to hunt. Chances are your bird has had a bad experience or two with hunters (maybe with you) and he is extremely leery of calling. The gobbler may be desperate for a hen, but it is likely he will stay put and gobble, trying to encourage her to come to him.

Catching the tom coming off the roost is the best tactic in this situation. Call very sparingly and stick with clucks. If the gobbler has been educated to calling, it was probably with the loud and constant yelps of an inexperienced hunter. Gobblers that haven't become hunter shy can be easy to call at this phase of the breeding cycle. Those that have will be tough to fool in every aspect of the hunt.

Suppose you're hunting a very wary bird. He won't come to your calls, but by now you may have his movements patterned. You can try posting in an area you know he frequents. Especially look for logging roads or trails going through thick undergrowth, and take a stand there before his expected time of arrival.

If a bird gobbles but seems afraid to approach your calling, try this: After he wanders away from his initial position, sneak

Photo by Charlie Farmer

When heavy hunting pressure is a problem, it can often pay off to travel deep into inaccessible country to hunt your turkey.

over to exactly where he was and try calling from there. Shy birds feel safer returning to a place they've just been.

This may be a good time to canoe into some untrekked turkey country, or get the gate key to some unhunted private land. An uneducated gobbler is most vulnerable at this stage. And if you don't have a turkey by now, it's time to try something new!

Other Spring Techniques

Often the most difficult part of spring hunting is getting the gobbler to come those last few yards into shooting range. Increasing numbers of hunters are finding that lifelike turkey hen decoys are a very effective solution to the problem. Though wary of what they hear, gobblers seem to think seeing is believing. Hunters report that on many occasions gobblers will actually try to mate with the decoy (if they're allowed to get that far). Hen decoys can often place the gobbler exactly where you want to shoot, and will also hold a tom's attention, lessening the chances he will spot you.

Most hunters set up to call a gobbler with the decoy about 20 yards away in an area that offers a good shot. Decoys are also an advantage when setting up in an area where you hope to intercept a tom. Put the decoy in an area the bird frequents and where the gobbler can see the decoy from a good distance. This may be a logging road he crosses in his travels, or on the edge of a field where he commonly struts. Remember that decoys can be dangerous in some situations, and follow all safety precautions outlined in other chapters.

Another special technique for hunting spring gobblers is the buddy system. Two hunters working together can use different and more productive methods for fooling a wise old bird. If you have problems with a tom hanging up, one hunter can set up and call while the other—the gunner—gets closer and tries to intercept the bird on his way in. In some cases hunting partners can work a system that moves birds from one hunter to the other.

Hunters working together often have problems communicating. Work out a system of signals—preferably signals made with turkey, crow, or owl calls. Keep in mind that when hunting with a partner, there is a greater chance of the tom spotting you, and there is a greater chance for an accident. Hunt very deliberately.

Hunting Subordinate Birds

Subordinate male turkeys include jakes and the weaker, less-aggressive gobblers. They behave quite differently from the dominant gobblers, and require a slightly different hunting approach.

Photo by Mike Strandlund

Photo by Roy E. Decker

A turkey decoy puts the gobbler's awesome eyesight to work for you. The results can be amazing; a tom very leery of your calling may drop all defenses when he spots your bogus bird.

Top Right
The buddy system, with one caller and one shooter, may turn the tables on a turkey. When hunting close to a friend, you must pay extra attention to concealment and caution.

Photo by Mike Strandlund

In most cases, being less experienced or genetically inferior birds, they are easier to hunt.

Male turkeys without harems during the breeding season are lonely, anxious, and frustrated. This contributes to their tendency to answer the call of a single hen. At the same time, they are fearful that a dominant gobbler will catch them with the hen, which discourages them from responding. For the same reason, they gobble rarely.

When jakes are around and you want to hunt them exclusively, make your calls loud and often. Since they probably won't be spooked by this type of calling, as a smart gobbler might, the important thing is that you get their attention and keep it. They may come in quickly and silently, perhaps in a group, looking for a quick session with the hen before a gobbler arrives. Jakes often respond best to the gobbles and lower-pitched yelps of other jakes. The raspy call of an older hen may attract jakes looking for either a mate or a "mother figure."

When you're after jakes or gobblers, cluck and yelp intermittently. If you heard a gobble nearby, the jake will probably be afraid to answer your calls anyway, and you're better off using the subtle approach of gobbler hunting.

Making the Shot

If you've done everything right, you'll find yourself in the heart-stopping position of looking at a strutting turkey within shooting range. Your gun or bow is poised for the shot.

But wait; there are more considerations. Are you sure that's really a gobbler? Seeing him gobble or strut, you can be sure. But if the turkey came walking in, you have to look closer. Most states allow hunters to shoot any bearded turkey. Look hard for the beard. Even though you see the beard, you may recognize the bird as a hen. Conservation-minded hunters will pass up the shot, satisfied that their knowledge and responsibility allowed an entire family of young turkeys to live.

If you do recognize the bird as a gobbler, hold out for a sure shot. Wait until the tom is well within range. If you're in a bad position to get your gun on the bird and shoot, wait. Avoid trying to "outdraw" a turkey—it will invariably be in the air or ducking behind a tree when the shot gets there, and there is too good a chance of wounding the bird.

Don't move until the turkey's head is hidden, so you can point unseen. When there is little chance of the gobbler putting an obstruction between you and him, wait until the bird is strutting away from you, with his tail hiding his head. Then move the gun into shooting position and ease the safety off. Be conscious that the safety is off, and remember to put it back on after you shoot or if you don't get a shot.

Photo by Roy E. Decker

This is where the hunt ends. If you can make the shot with only the movement of one finger, this turkey is yours. If the bead's not on his head at this point, the only reward will be a rude education— for both of you.

Before pulling the trigger, scan the ground between you and the turkey for brush and other pellet obstructions. You may have to refocus your eyes to see those small branches and briars that can destroy a pattern.

When it's time to shoot, your only movement should be a deliberate pressing of the trigger. Wait until the gobbler's head

Photo Courtesy of Missouri Department of Conservation

When making your final move to shooting position, wait until the gobbler's head is behind a tree. Beware that the movement is not picked up by another turkey in the area, which might signal danger to your target.

125

is extended—not pulled into his chest while strutting—before you take a shot. An outstretched neck makes for a bigger target. You may prompt him into extending his neck by giving one sharp cluck just when you are ready to press the trigger; some hunters actually bid their bird farewell.

With a shotgun, hold for the center or base of the neck. If you miss your first shot, the turkey will make a frantic attempt to escape. Shoot again only if you're close enough for an effective body shot. You'll have to lead and follow through on a fast-moving target. If the turkey gets to marginal range before you can get off a second shot, shoot only if you're sure he was wounded by your first pellet charge. Chances are his head and neck will be protected by his body or by obstructions as he departs.

Recovering Wounded Turkeys

Ideally, a hunter is skilled with his firearm or bow, is a good judge of shoot or don't-shoot situations, and makes instant kills when he does pull the trigger or release the string. But if there is a miscalculation, the turkey may be wounded and attempt an escape. It is then the hunter's responsibility to make every effort to recover the bird, because even a slightly injured bird may die later as a result of its wounds.

If the turkey dashes off after you shoot, quickly note its position at the shot, then follow the bird quickly and carefully. The closer you can stay, the farther you can follow the turkey to determine where it's going. Turkeys seldom leave good blood trails, and it may be necessary to see it fall or actually find it dead. If you lose track of the turkey, go back to the point of the hit and look for feathers and a blood trail.

If the turkey flies off, listen. The bird may die in flight and fall with a thud. It may become weak and land in a short distance. Mark the spot and get there quickly.

Thoroughly search the area where a wounded turkey could be. Look under logs and in thick brush; wounded turkeys often hole up. Dogs are a great aid in recovering wounded turkeys.

CHAPTER 7

HUNTING FALL TURKEYS

Though fall lacks the thrills of hair-raising encounters with a hot spring gobbler, the hunt is more challenging. Fall birds are more abundant and hens are usually open game, but turkeys are harder to locate. One does not merely stroll through the woods and call one into shooting range. Techniques change according to:

- **Available Foods**
- **Composition of the Flock**
- **Weather**
- **Terrain**

Photo by Mike Strandlund

Turkey hunting in fall varies considerably from spring gobbler hunting. Search for flocks around food sources such as powerline corridors. Since birds are harder to locate, it may help for hunters to spread out, find some birds, then come together to hunt the flock.

As in spring gobbler hunting, a hunter must use his knowledge of turkey habits, woodsmanship, and calling. Careful scouting is necessary to find wild turkeys consistently any time of year. Yet in fall, the hunter must use perseverance and cunning, and search for turkeys all day—sometimes all season. It puts the hunt into a whole new perspective.

Fall Foods

Food availability is the main factor to consider when looking for turkeys in fall and winter. In different localities and at different stages of autumn, birds concentrate on different food types. In Vermont, fall turkeys may be found around harvested lowland cornfields. In West Virginia, the birds prefer high mountain flats lush with ripe wild grapes and cherries. In Texas, the early fall hunter may find dense turkey populations around fields filled with grasshoppers. In Pennsylvania, acorns and beechnuts are preferred foods. California's pinyon pine and poison oaks, dropping seeds and berries, will attract turkeys.

Early in the fall, ripe poke berries and other weed seeds are plentiful, particularly where gypsymoth caterpillars or other forest pests have defoliated the forest. Various fruits and seeds fall to the ground as the season progresses, and turkeys will scratch for them. Green sprouts and insects are also eagerly sought in fall. Any field with crops and insect life, surrounded by good turkey territory, is a likely place to look for fall flocks. Check the edges of such fields for feathers and droppings, and scope the area from a distance looking for birds.

Feeding Sign

When feeding on fallen nuts and berries, turkeys leave telltale scratchings in the forest's leafy carpet. Turkey scratchings are very obvious, as a flock can feed across nearly 1,000 acres daily, leaving hundreds of piles of leaves and bare spots.

A single scratching will be the shape of a V or an oval, 12 to 18 inches in diameter, with almost all the leaves removed from the center. Check for scratchings at the bases of oaks and other trees that drop mast foods. Turkeys scratch here for acorns and insects found in the damp, shaded soil. Examine the sign for freshness by lifting some undisturbed leaves nearby. Compare the newly exposed leaves with the turkey scratchings. If both are equally damp, the scratchings are probably fresh.

The turkey's direction of travel can be ascertained by the way the leaves are piled. Turkeys walk forward as they feed, so leaves will be piled to the rear of the scratch marks. While deer also feed by pawing back leaves in search of food, they usually do not feed in a specific direction, and their pawings tend to pile leaves at random as they feed. Deer rarely scratch down to the topsoil as turkeys do. If the hunter finds many hoofprints and droppings at a suspected feeding site, he can assume much of the work was done by deer. Unlike deer, turkeys scratch hard under logs and along old fencerows in search of grubs and other

Photo by Mike Strandlund

When feeding in woods, turkeys leave scratchings that tell you when they came through and where they were going. Concentrate your search for scratchings beneath trees that drop mast foods like acorns and nuts.

Photo by Mike Strandlund

Forest floor scratchings can point out turkey flock activity.

insects. If you find this type of scratching, the sign was left by turkeys.

You can sometimes follow scratchings, stopping to call occasionally, until a bird answers and gives away the location of the flock. Then plan your hunting strategy.

Water can also be a prime location for turkey sign. Be aware of locations of spring seeps, riverbottoms, runoffs, and puddles. Check here for tracks in the mud.

Flock Composition

Knowledge of the turkey's fall flocking habits is a must in planning your hunt. You are most likely to encounter a single family unit—a hen with her brood of the year. However, you may also see large mixed flocks, some as large as 50 birds, comprised of mother hens, poults, barren hens, toms, and jakes. Later in the season, jakes split away from their mothers and sisters into flocks of their own. Adult gobblers tend to gather in all-male flocks and offer the fall hunter his greatest challenge. You can determine flock composition by studying droppings among the scratchings. Small, round droppings indicate hens and young birds; larger, J-shaped feces are left by gobblers.

Sometimes young birds are quite noisy; the astute turkey hunter will locate as many or more birds by sound as by sight. Aside from their calls, fall birds make a variety of sounds that can alert the attentive hunter.

A dozen or more birds walking and scratching through dry leaves can be heard from 150 yards or more on a calm day. They sound like a group of deer or people walking and feeding, except turkeys rarely snap twigs or branches. Some birds scratch and search for food constantly, creating a continuous shuffling and dragging noise.

NRA Staff Photo

You can determine whether it is a flock of gobblers or hens and young that you are following by studying droppings found among tracks or scratch marks.

Flocks of turkeys flying from or to the roost make a loud flapping of wings audible for quite a distance. In fall, turkeys are also very vocal early and late in the day.

Young birds from a family flock are the easiest to hunt. They readily come to a call when in need of companionship, and can be still-hunted in many situations. Fall gobblers are the hardest of all turkeys to hunt.

Weather

When choosing your hunting method for a given day, consider weather conditions. During dry weather, the best prescription is more sitting and less walking. While the footsteps of a person and a wild turkey sound the same to us, a bird will often be gone long before he sees the hunter if he hears something suspicious. Sitting allows you to listen for approaching birds.

Rainy or windy weather hampers the fall turkey hunter. While you can move with less chance of being seen, calling carries a

Photo by Leonard Lee Rue III

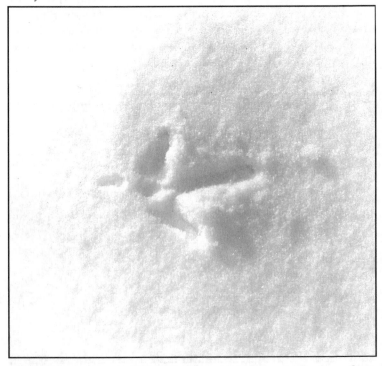

After a new snow, give the turkeys a couple hours to fly down from their roosts and make tracks. This is the easiest way to locate a fall flock.

Photo by Mike Strandlund

relatively short distance. Move more often and call with greater volume. On dark, rainy days birds stay on the roost longer, and when on the ground, avoid thickets where they can be soaked from brushing against wet vegetation. They do not call from the roost on dark days as often as they do in good weather.

In late fall, stay on the move and watch for tracks and scratchings. When there is snow cover, trailing a flock in snow is quite easy, but be sure to watch as far ahead as possible. Birds are extra wary in snow. Don't be discouraged if you can't get into the woods at the break of day on snowy mornings. By giving the birds an hour or two to fly down and make a few tracks, you increase your chance to encounter fresh sign.

During very clear, cold weather, turkeys are most apt to be found on sunlit, south-facing slopes or other areas that are warmer than the surroundings. In fog, turkeys rely on vocal communication more and eyesight less. Turkeys, though harder to find, can be easier to call in thick fog.

Terrain

The wild turkey has adapted to many types of habitat regardless of terrain. You may find the bird on the steepest mountain or the flattest bottomland. Turkeys use the lay of the land for defense, but a hunter can also use terrain to his advantage. Once you've determined a flock's intended line of travel, use ground features to cover movements as you flank or swing ahead of the birds. Also, fall turkeys seem to habitually use certain hollows, saddles, benches, or riverbottoms for travel routes. Open terrain dictates different tactics than thicker, brushier areas. Turkeys often travel along paths or logging roads through thickets.

Fall Hunting Tactics

Turkeys, like some other upland gamebirds, have a strong flocking instinct. When turkeys become separated from the main flock, they urgently try to rejoin their companions, calling in an attempt to locate each other. The most common fall hunting technique is scattering or breaking up a turkey flock, then calling in a lone bird that is trying to get back with the group. This method offers the fall hunter the greatest chance of success.

Once you locate a flock, the real fun begins. If you have a moment, observe the flock and try to see if it is comprised of hens and young birds, gobblers, or mixed turkeys. How close can you stalk the flock, and what is the time of day?

Scatter the Flock

Using cover and terrain to your advantage, get as close as possible. Use underbrush and small rises to conceal your stalk, and try to get uphill of the birds so you can dash faster and scatter them downhill. Then break up the flock by running toward it and shouting, possibly shooting into the air, but being very careful. Don't try to shoot a bird at this point; very rarely can you get a sure shot in this situation. Try to frighten the flock as much as possible so birds panic and fly or run in all directions. After awhile, the turkeys will feel it's safe to reassemble, locating each other with calls.

Photo by Mike Strandlund

Dashing at a flock to scatter the birds, then calling as they try to get together, is the surest way to take a fall turkey. Be careful you don't stumble and have a gun accident.

Birds that are alone are the easiest to call back. If the birds were not badly scared and did not scatter individually in all directions, chances for calling success are slim. Birds may stay together in small bunches and not try to regroup for several hours.

At this point, set up in a safe, comfortable position where you have a good view. Remain absolutely still and quiet to give the birds a chance to calm down. If the birds stay in small groups as they fly away, pursue one group until you break it up.

Some birds will call five minutes after a flock is split; others are quiet for an hour or more. Don't give up—remain on your stand, possibly two hours or more, provided you are certain the flock was well separated.

If the birds you busted appear to be a family flock, and you hear a coarse-voiced turkey begin calling, it is probably the

The flock-scattering technique works best if turkeys are badly scared and fly or run off in all directions. Single turkeys get lonely soon; anxious for companionship, they usually come quickly to a call. If they aren't frightened, they may go off in small groups and be very difficult to call back.

mother hen trying to assemble her young. This bird will be very difficult to call. Some hunters believe the flock hen should not be shot, because it makes the young birds more vulnerable to hunters and other threats. If you feel you can't or don't want to shoot the flock hen, get up immediately and reflush her. Otherwise, the woods may become silent in a few minutes, indicating the flock has come together and your opportunity has vanished.

Scaring the flock hen off, your chance of calling a young bird to the gun is much better. Don't use the adult hen call at this time unless you're an expert; the young birds are attuned to the sound of their mother and can easily identify a fraud. Concentrate instead on the kee-kee run, lost call, purrs, or clucks that imitate a young turkey.

Calling Birds Back
Listen for the sounds of calling turkeys and try to match the pitch and pattern of their calls. The call you're most apt to hear is the kee-kee run. A few minutes after you have set up, begin

calling softly in case birds are very near. Gradually increase the volume and momentum of your calls. Give a series of calls every minute or so. Call in several directions, so all the birds can locate the source of the sound. Pause often and long to search the woods with your eyes and ears for approaching birds. If you see a bird coming your way, he may have your calls pinpointed and should keep coming. Remain quiet and still, in shooting position, as the bird comes near. If it veers off, give a couple clucks or yelps to regain its attention. If one bird spooks, keep calling; the others may not have been tipped off.

Photo by Mike Strandlund

Call fall turkeys in the same setup as spring hunting—gun up, back against a tree, and as still as possible.

Flocks broken up late in the day tend to wait until morning before reassembling. They will roost individually. Wait at the break-up site until dark, then leave, marking your trail so you can return before light next morning. Scattering a flock just before or just after they go to roost, then returning to call next morning, is the most successful approach to this tactic.

Hard-hunted birds generally talk very little and take longer to regroup. If they have been flushed several times, they often return slowly to the break point with little or no calling. If you hunt popular public areas, the birds will be more cooperative later in the season after the crowds have gone.

If the flock consists of mature gobblers, you'll need hunting and calling strategy different than for young birds. Pleading kee-kee runs will likely be unanswered. Most old birds will not call for at least an hour or two after the flush. If they do call, listen for one or two deep clucks, or a throaty yelp or two, every 15 or 20 minutes. Answer with similar calls, making them sound raspy, cautious, and only semi-interested. Hunting old autumn gobblers requires the ultimate woodsman's knowledge. The odds for bagging a longbeard are better if you follow some time-tested techniques.

Photo by Glenn "Tink" Smith

Hunting fall gobblers is the toughest challenge in turkey hunting. Unlike springtime, they are not distracted by the need to breed. They will come very slowly and deliberately to the call in fall.

Mature gobblers seeking companions are not in any hurry. Only very occasional, deep calling can bring one to the gun. Clucks, yelps, or even an occasional gobble help lure them, but patience is most valuable now. The duel may take two or three hours. It's tough, but remaining absolutely motionless on your stand for several hours is your best hunting technique for this situation. Gobblers scattered during the afternoon may not try to reassemble until the following morning. If flushed in mountainous terrain, old gobblers tend to regroup on higher ground, so locate your calling site accordingly.

Still-Hunting

Developing the skills to walk quietly through the forest, using the vegetation and natural land features to hide from prying eyes and ears, will help you bag fall turkeys. So will the ability to read turkey sign in order to locate and track turkeys.

Avoiding the turkey's keen hearing and eyesight is the key to this technique. When hunting hilly country, use tops or ridgelines to sneak and peek down the slopes. On lower flatbacks and valleys, approach every depression or rise with care. Use cover to follow the direction of scratchings. Listen for feeding activity, rustling of forest litter, and the chatter of a content flock of turkeys. Look for uplifted leaves, the motion of a feeding turkey, or the round, dark backs of a group of birds. Once you have located turkeys, analyze the situation, watch the birds, and decide on your game plan. You might be able to tell from the sounds and movements which way the flock is heading. Keep in mind that in mixed habitat, the flock will likely follow the route that offers the best visibility. Then, using all cover to your advantage, move into position to await a clear shot or dash into and break up the flock.

It can be almost impossible to flush turkeys if they know you are following. The old "sneak around and head 'em off" tactic works when you can anticipate their direction of travel. Being very familiar with the area and the workings of a turkey's mind, you might be able to guess where the flock will go, circle in front of them, and simply wait. Or you can set up in their probable path and call.

The most popular and perhaps best method of hunting turkeys with the rifle is quietly still-hunting. While it may be almost impossible to sneak within shotgun range of turkeys, a careful stalker can rather easily sneak within rifle range. This may be done by easing over a ridge and scanning the draw below; glass-

Still-hunting is popular with rifle hunters in fall. With a quiet approach, a good marksman can walk within range of a turkey flock.

ing fields or other open areas to locate and start a stalk on a flock; or simply strolling through the woods, stopping, looking, and listening. Try to stay completely out of sight during the stalk, then ease into shooting position. Get a solid rest with your rifle and wait for a still shot.

Posting

Fall turkeys, especially gobblers or birds with lots of food available, may establish travel patterns within relatively small areas. If you do your homework, you may find a good place to post (sit and wait quietly) and intercept a flock on its daily routine.

The rifle gives hunters an advantage if they hunt by posting, by sniping turkeys at longer distances in open country, or by still-hunting. Rifles are generally less effective and more dangerous than shotguns when calling, however.

In areas where turkey and deer seasons coincide, posting is a favorite technique for rifle hunters. The hunter uses a blind or treestand in an area where he knows turkeys travel. Stillness is the critical factor, especially if deer season is on and you are wearing blaze orange. If you do wear orange, you can make a blind that completely hides you, but beware of situations in which you should make yourself visible to other hunters. Blinds are illegal for turkey hunting in some states.

Photos by Mike Strandlund

With a good knowledge of the travel patterns of a certain flock, a shotgunner or bowhunter can be successful on turkeys in fall. Posting is the favorite method of hunters after both deer and turkeys.

Other Fall Tactics

You may also call to a small, undisturbed flock or single bird. These may be turkeys you spotted or birds you happen across by roaming and calling. Use the same technique in setting up as prescribed for spring gobbler hunting. Sit at the base of a tree or other large natural object, gun up, staying alert and ready, and give an occasional call. The wild turkey is a curious, social creature and may seek out other turkeys' calls at any time.

When no flock magically appears after you enter the woods, you may have to work very hard to find turkeys. Be alert for single birds or small groups flushed by other hunters. An excellent technique is to sit and call for a half hour or more, then move a couple hundred yards and repeat the process. Most of the time small turkey groups will at least answer a lost call (kee-kee run). If you hear birds but cannot get them to come, you have probably located a flock. Circle in front of them until you can call again, get a shot, or rush, flush and separate them.

Hunting from a stand or blind overlooking plots of crops attractive to turkeys is common in the South. It is quite productive, but not legal everywhere. Again, patience plays a big part in this waiting game.

Photos by Mike Strandlund

Some fall turkey hunters have good success using a trained dog. The dog must range widely in search of a flock, then bust the birds and stay stone-still while the hunter calls one back. The dog may retrieve the bird, and is most helpful in tracking a wounded turkey.

Hunting with Dogs

In some states, hunting turkeys with a dog in fall is legal and traditional. For a bird dog owner, this adds an interesting dimension to turkey hunting. The dog must be wide ranging, well disciplined, and able to work well with its hunting party. Ideally, a turkey dog will locate a flock by scent, then trail and eventually scatter the flock. Upon breaking up the flock, the dog will remain at the point of flush, barking. Once the hunter has located his canine companion, he will call to the separated birds while the dog remains quiet and camouflaged at his side. After the bird is called in and shot, the dog will retrieve it. Traditionally, spaniels, setters, and pointers have been trained as turkey dogs; just about any hunting breed will do.

Keep in mind that being a successful fall turkey hunter requires experience. Fall hunting techniques are not quickly mastered, and there are always things to learn each season.

Part III

The Complete Turkey Hunter

Photo by Mike Strandlund

CHAPTER 8

TURKEY TROPHIES AND TABLEFARE

A wild turkey's role as a valuable resource does not end at the climax of a successful hunt. Turkeys provide beautiful trophies and terrific tablefare with little expense and effort.

Field Care

Turkey feathers and meat can easily be damaged. As soon as you shoot and see the bird go down, you must begin taking care of them.

Most times after an instantly fatal shot from a shotgun, turkeys flap their wings violently for several seconds. Mortally wounded birds may try to fly or run. Get to the bird quickly to prevent a possible escape and to keep the turkey from damaging its feathers by breakage and blood stains.

NRA Staff Photo

The magnificent wild turkey gobbler is one of the forest's finest trophies and a prized wild food. To fully appreciate the rewards of your hunt, care well for your turkey.

Dispatch a wounded bird by a blow or foot pressure to the head. Then pin the turkey to the ground with its wings in place, being very careful of sharp spurs, and hold the bird until the struggling subsides. This keeps feathers from being broken, you from being injured, and other hunters from taking a shot at thrashing wings. Allow blood to drain from the mouth or the wound, then wrap with absorbent material to keep blood from getting on feathers.

Entrails should be removed soon unless the weather is cool or you plan on taking the bird directly to a taxidermist. Simply make an incision between the tail and the tip of the breastbone (the same way chickens are cleaned) and pull out the innards,

Photo by Michael Hanback

In warm weather, turkeys should be cleaned immediately to prevent spoilage. It's not necessary if the weather is cool, and it shouldn't be done if you're planning to have a full body mount of your bird.

trying not to break them. You may remove the crop by slitting the skin between the neck and breast. Save the heart, liver, and gizzard (don't forget to split the gizzard and remove its inner lining before cooking it). Wipe out the body cavity and absorb any fluids that have gotten on feathers. Use a paper towel or cloth, or an absorbent substance like cornmeal. Don't use corn starch—it can get stuck in the feathers and ruin their iridescence. Keep the bird cool during transport. Don't let feathers get wet or matted down.

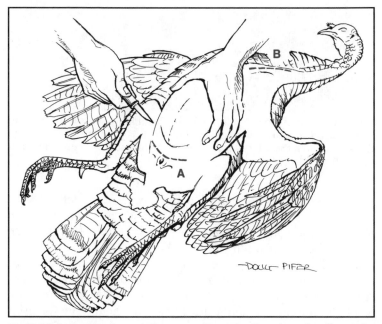

To field dress a turkey, make a cut shown by line A and pull out the innards. Remove the crop (undigested food) with an incision at line B. Wipe the exposed areas clean and protect them from flies.

Preserving the Moment

Among the best turkey hunting trophies you can have are good photographs of the hunt and its result. When you're frustrated by lean hunting times or can't hunt anymore, a good photo collection can help you relive your glory days.

If you want top-quality pictures or enlargements, a 35mm camera is a must. The newer autofocus cameras are a good choice, enabling amateur photographers to get very good pictures. They are convenient to carry and some have small, built-in

Photo by Mike Strandlund

Photographs of favorite hunts will be invaluable to you in years to come. Good 35mm camera gear, selected for your specific applications, provides the best compromise between quality, economy, and versatility.

flash systems for pictures in low light. Single-lens reflex (SLR) cameras can give even better quality, but they take more expertise to operate. If you get a camera with a self-timer, you can take photos of yourself when you're alone.

The best color enlargements come from slide film with a low ASA (light sensitivity) rating, such as Kodachrome 64. Higher ASA film such as 200 or 400 allows you to take pictures with less light, but quality diminishes. The same holds true for print film—the best choice if you want a large number of smaller prints for a photo album.

In taking pictures, do all you can for technical quality. Try to put your subject in good light without harsh shadows. Set up the pictures for aesthetic appeal and include all elements important to the moment—you, your turkey, the habitat, friends, camp scenes, etc.

If you're interested in photographing wild turkeys (a great preseason activity) you'll need a high-quality camera, a telephoto lens of at least 200mm, skills to use them well, and lots of luck. Select a low-ASA color slide film or 400 ASA black & white film.

A few hints for better pictures: focus carefully, keep your subject in the best light, make sure your shutter speed is fast enough, take time to compose your pictures, and mind details.

The Turkey as Trophy

Turkeys make great trophies, whether you choose an attractive wall hanging that's easy to make yourself, or an awesome, full-body-mounted gobbler in strutting, flying, or gobbling position.

You can "score" your turkey similar to the way other big game animals are scored. The National Wild Turkey Federation uses this formula: Add the live weight of the bird (pounds) plus two times the beard length (inches) plus 10 times the length of each spur. A typical 18-pound gobbler with a six-inch beard and one-inch spurs would score 50 points.

Photo by Michael Hanback

Most hunters are interested in the weight of their turkey and the length of the spurs and beard. You can plug this data into a formula developed by the National Wild Turkey Federation to see how your gobbler ranks as a trophy.

Full Body Mounts

Taxidermists can create just about any position you desire for your mounted gobbler. Standing or strutting mounts are designed for tabletop display, while flying poses are usually hung from a wall or ceiling. Keep in mind they take up considerable space, and decide beforehand where the mount will be placed so you can have it positioned accordingly.

Check with a taxidermist or two before hunting. They may have special requirements, such as needing the bird delivered unfrozen with entrails intact. In most cases, however, a small cut for field dressing will make no difference, and the bird may be delivered frozen. Ask the taxidermist if he can save the meat from the turkey for you.

A full-body mount is the most striking turkey trophy. Walking, strutting, and flying are favorite positions.

Photo Courtesy of Missouri Department of Conservation

Beautiful wallhanging trophies are easy and inexpensive to make yourself. Skin the gobbler, flesh out the pelt, and treat it with drying compound.

Wallhanging Trophies

A full-body gobbler mount is spectacular, but it may cost $300 or more. You can make a very appealing wallhanging trophy yourself for virtually no expense. These trophies can be a simple beard and tail display or a large plaque with tail, back, and wing feathers.

For a simple tailfeather trophy, cut the tail off close to the body, making sure you don't damage the quill ends. Trim the flesh and fat from the tail base, cover it with borax or a similar drying substance. Be sure to cut out the oil gland as it can spoil the mount. Fan the tail out into a half-circle, and secure it that way to dry. Be sure it is out of reach of insects and animals.

When dry, remove the borax, trim off ragged pieces, and make any other preparations you want. Some hunters attach the tail to a plaque, or cover the rather unsightly base of the tail. Most times the beard is also displayed with the tail.

The colorful feathers of a turkey's back also add to the trophy, and many hunters include them all in the wallhanging.

153

If you go this route, you must first skin the turkey:

1) Hang the turkey by the head or feet, or lay flat on a table.
2) Cut the tail free from the body, leaving it attached to the back skin.
3) Cut the skin along each side of the body, following the natural divisions between the feathers. Make your cut over each wing and end your cut at the base of the neck.
4) Pull the skin off over the neck, as you would pull off a glove inside out.

Remove as much fat and flesh as possible from the skin. Wings, if you want to preserve them, must be fleshed out completely. Then cover the entire skin with drying agent. Stretch it out to the form you want, and tack it to cardboard or plywood. Put it in a safe, dry place. After a couple weeks you can remove the skin from the drying board, trim and clean it, and hang it or place it on a plaque.

There are many variations on this method of trophy making. You can use the complete outer body except for the head—including the feet. You can leave the wings on, discard them, or display them separately, with their butts together, in a large butterfly shape.

Other Turkey Trophies

The length of a gobbler's beard is considered by some to be the measure of a turkey hunter's success. These coarse, hair-like feathers are a favorite souvenir and seldom discarded. To preserve the beard, simply cut it off behind the skin and flesh at the base, dry the base, then coat it with paraffin or epoxy to keep bristles from pulling out.

Preserved gobbler feet, complete with spurs, are interesting. Some hunters save feet by cutting the leg off at the feather line and weighting or nailing it into an upright position so it stands flat-footed when dry. Cover the cut-off end with feathers or wrappings to make it more attractive.

Other souvenirs you can make from parts of your turkey include necklaces and other jewelry, made with feathers, spurs, and beards. Turkey feathers are a beautiful addition to dry-flower bouquets and similar crafts. Wing feathers are perfect fletching for the arrows of traditional archers, and body feathers are used by tiers of fishing flies. Wingbones may be fashioned into turkey calls.

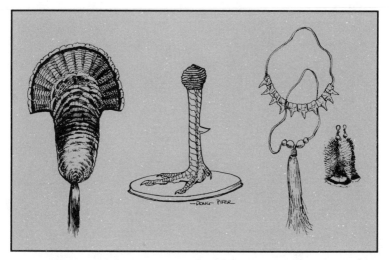

Popular souvenirs from bagged turkeys include preserved tail fans and backs; dried gobbler feet; beards; and jewelry made from feathers, spurs, and beards.

Care of the Trophy

Turkey trophies should be placed carefully so that just the right amount of light at just the right angle brings out the multicolored iridescence in the feathers. Indirect sunlight is best--keep the trophy out of direct sunlight or the feather colors may fade.

Your mounts need other care and maintenance: Fumigate them annually to prevent damage from carpet beetles and other insects; wipe clean any oil that appears on the mount; dust periodically to keep dirt from penetrating feathers and ruining the colors.

Turkey as Tablefare

A symbol of bounty and providence, turkey has been a revered American food since 1621, when four wild turkeys served as centerpiece for a famous feast at Plymouth Colony, Massachusetts.

Modern pilgrims are still thankful for the incomparably mellow taste of wild turkey. It is a favorite among wild game connoisseurs no matter how it is prepared, though the overwhelming favorite recipe is roasting. Often a stuffing is prepared, preferably with wild ingredients such as wild rice or chestnuts, though it can be good roasted with just an apple and onion inside the body cavity to impart flavor. Most cooks prefer not to complicate the turkey's soft flavor with fancy recipes calling for marinades

155

Photo by Mike Strandlund

Steeped in tradition, roast wild turkey is only one of the many delicious recipes possible with the mellow-flavored meat of the wild turkey.

and lots of spices. Keep it simple. There are many good wild turkey recipes; here are a few.

Roast Wild Turkey

1 wild turkey, dressed
2 medium onions, skinned
1 teaspoon flour
4 strips bacon
½ stick of butter or margarine
1 cooking bag
2 medium apples, skinned
1 tablespoon pepper
½ tablespoon salt
spices

Dress the bird and preferably pluck; it may be skinned if you want to save the pelt. Stuff with butter or margarine, onions and apples, close the opening, salt and pepper the bird, and lay the strips of bacon across the breast. Place the turkey, flour, and spices in the cooking bag, shake, and close the bag. Roast the bird at 325–350 degrees for 15–25 minutes per pound, depending on the age and toughness of the bird (older birds need more cooking).

Wild Rice Dressing

Chopped giblets
¼ cup butter
¼ cup chopped onions
¼ cup tomato paste
1 cup wild rice
¼ cup chopped celery
1 tablespoon chopped green pepper
½ cup mushrooms

Bring four cups of water to a boil; stir in the giblets and wild rice. Simmer until tender, about a half hour, and drain. Keep hot. In a skillet, melt the butter and saute the celery, green pepper, and mushrooms for about three minutes. Mix all the ingredients. Makes about four cups.

Sauteed Turkey Breast

**Turkey breast meat
1 teaspoon salt
1 cup flour
¼ cup butter
1 teaspoon pepper**

Fillet the turkey breast meat from the carcass and cut into steaks about ¼ to ½ inch thick. Salt and flour the steaks, and saute them in the butter for only a minute or so. These sauteed breast steaks are juicy and flavorful without a hint of gaminess. Use the remaining meat for the following recipe.

Creamy Turkey Noodle Soup

**3 or 4 pounds cooked or uncooked turkey parts
2 cups thickly sliced carrots
1 cup sliced celery
1 clove garlic
¾ cup flour
salt and pepper
3 cups milk
1 cup chopped green pepper
¾ cup chopped onion
1 pound egg noodles
4 tablespoons butter or margarine**

Bring water to a boil and add turkey parts, simmering until meat falls from the bone. Remove bones and add all ingredients *except* noodles, flour, butter, and 1 cup milk. Cook until vegetables start to tenderize. Add noodles and cook until almost done. In a bowl, mix flour and remaining milk; add to soup and boil for three minutes. Stir in butter or margarine, and season to taste. Serves an average size turkey camp.

CHAPTER 9
SAFETY AND ETHICS IN TURKEY HUNTING

S hooting sports as a whole have a surprisingly low accident rate compared with other outdoor activities. But while it's true that hunting is statistically safer than football or swimming or even tennis, there is one fact that all turkey hunters

Photo Courtesy Missouri Department of Conservation

The nature of turkey hunting, combined with carelessness by a few hunters, have made it the most accident-prone type of hunting in America. A common cause of accidents is one hunter mistaking another for game—most likely when the potential victim is openly carrying a decoy or dead turkey.

must keep in mind: Their sport ranks as the most dangerous of all hunting.

Consider these incidents:

• Dawn in the mountains of West Virginia. An anxious hunter glimpses a dark, bobbing object that appears to be a walking turkey. He fires his shotgun at the target, which turns out to be the face of another hunter. The man is blinded permanently.

• Two Arkansas hunters enter the woods and split up. One spots what he believes is the white head of a gobbler, shoots his crossbow, and hits his mark. He walks over to find his companion, dead, an arrow in his chest where his white T-shirt was exposed.

• In New England, a turkey hunter in light cotton clothing is lost in the mountains when an early-spring snowstorm hits. That night, wet, cold, and with no way to build a fire, he freezes to death.

• On a western hunt, a rifleman takes a shot at a turkey, misses, but hits and seriously injures another hunter on the next ridge.

These anecdotes are not meant to frighten, but to show where carelessness on a hunting trip can lead. The possibility of accidents and how to prevent them should always be on a hunter's mind. A person conscious of danger and careful to take all safety precautions will never cause a hunting accident.

Firearm Safety
Safety in hunting begins with safe handling of firearms. These rules for safety in handling and shooting apply to all firearms:

Photo by Mike Strandlund

Turkeys already have a great advantage over you in hearing and eyesight. Protect what you have by wearing ear protectors and safety glasses while target shooting.

1. Always have control of the gun's muzzle and keep it pointed in a safe direction.
2. Be positive of your target's identity before shooting.
3. Be prepared and take time to fire a safe shot. If unsure, or if you must rush so you cannot mount the gun correctly, pass up the shot. If there is any doubt whether you should shoot—don't.
4. Use the right ammunition for your firearm. Carry only one type of ammo to ensure you don't mix different types. A 20-gauge shell loaded into a 12-gauge will slide into the barrel and lodge there. If a 12-gauge shell is loaded behind it and fired, the results can be disastrous.
5. If you fall, control the muzzle. After a fall, unload and check for dirt and damage and make sure the barrel is free of obstructions.
6. Unload your gun before attempting to climb a steep bank or traveling across hazardous terrain.

Turkey hunting requires that you follow all rules for safe gun handling, such as opening your action and setting your gun down before crossing a fence, or handing it to another hunter.

7. When you are alone and must cross a fence, unload your firearm and place it under the fence with the muzzle pointed away from yourself. When hunting with others and you must cross a fence or similar obstacle, unload the gun and keep the action open. Have one of your companions hold the gun while you cross. Then take their unloaded guns so your companions may cross safely.

8. Maintain your firearm, keep it clean, and never use a gun that is in poor condition, malfunctioning, or incapable of handling the ammunition you use. In cold weather, remove oil and grease from the gun so it cannot congeal and inhibit the action.

9. Be aware of the range of your pellets or bullets. Larger pellet loads can travel several hundred yards and bullets can travel over a mile. Make certain that your pellets cannot rain down on other hunters, and remember that shotgun pellets can ricochet off water, ground, and objects.

10. Adverse conditions and excitement can impair your mental and physical performance. Bulky clothing, rain, wind, snow, etc. can cause poor gun handling and reduce your concentration on safety. Fatigue can cause carelessness and clumsiness, as can the excitement of a bird coming in. For maximum safety, control these conditions as much as possible.

11. Be conscious of switching your gun's safety off, and remember to place it back on after the shooting opportunity has passed.

12. Establish zones of fire when hunting next to companions. Be sure your gun's muzzle is *always* pointing into your zone.

13. Alcohol, drugs, and hunting don't mix. Drugs and alcohol may impair your judgment; keen judgment is essential to safe hunting.

14. When you have finished hunting, unload your gun immediately and keep the action open.

15. If companions violate a rule of safe gun handling, bring it to their attention and refuse to hunt with them unless they correct their behavior.

Bow and Muzzleloader Safety

Bowhunters have similar safety rules to follow. Identifying the target and being sure of the background are also important before releasing an arrow. Broadheads must always be covered with an impenetrable shielding material, such as a padded, hard-plastic guard on a bow quiver. When walking, especially on steep or otherwise hazardous terrain, bowhunters should keep all arrows quivered in most situations. A fall on a sharp broadhead can be as dangerous as a gunshot wound.

If a turkey you shoot still has the arrow imbedded, be careful

Photo by Mike Strandlund

The muzzleloading turkey hunter must keep special safety considerations in mind. Use extreme care in loading and always wear safety glasses.

about approaching and grabbing the bird. It could flop, kick, or jump and stab you with an exposed broadhead.

Muzzleloader hunters have several special safety considerations. Black powder can cause a violent breech explosion with improper loads. Common causes of these include exceeding maximum powder charges; accidently loading double charges of powder and ball; using smokeless powder or the wrong type of black powder; and others.

Always stay clear of the muzzle as much as possible when loading. Carefully scribe marks on your ramrod to measure whether the gun is loaded. Handle powder and equipment carefully to avoid a fire. Get a book and take a course to thoroughly familiarize yourself with safe muzzleloading procedures before going hunting.

Handgunners must also take special precautions. A handgun's short barrel makes it more liable to point at yourself or someone else. Keep the gun securely holstered with the safety on, and be especially careful when moving the gun into or out of the holster. The hammer of a revolver should rest on an empty chamber.

Turkey Hunting Safety

While you may be familiar with the standard gun/bow safety requirements, there are special safety rules that apply to turkey hunting.

Most turkey hunting accidents happen when one hunter mistakes another for a turkey, or when a gun accidentally discharges and wounds the handler or someone nearby. The essential rules of hunting safety are to handle your gun with care and to identify your target positively before pulling the trigger. Keeping this in mind, and using common sense, will prevent the great majority of turkey hunting accidents.

Clothing

Turkey hunting safety begins before you even get dressed for the hunt. Never wear red, white, black, or light blue clothing that could be visible to another turkey hunter. These colors, the colors of a spring gobbler, may trigger an accident. An irresponsible hunter may think you are a turkey and point his gun or even shoot before identifying the target. When you are in full camo, a small bit of colored clothing appears to stand out by itself, with the rest of you invisible, and it can look surprisingly like a turkey head to a hunter who *wants* to see a turkey head. The colors may be especially dangerous if they are accompanied by other safety hazards, like gobbling calls or stalking.

Be very careful when carrying a bagged bird through the woods. It's best to use a large blaze orange bag or article of clothing in this situation.

Be careful about wearing white socks that may be exposed when you sit down; a white T-shirt exposed at the neck or exposed if you unbutton your shirt; a colored handkerchief that you might absent-mindedly pull out or let hang from a pocket.

A headnet and gloves, besides camouflaging you from the game, cover skin that might be mistaken for the white part of a gobbler.

Blaze Orange

More and more turkey hunters, realizing the dangers, are using blaze orange. It is seldom required by law, but should be worn whenever you are moving around--especially if you are carrying a bird. Turkeys are very difficult to stalk or walk up, so wearing blaze orange while walking has little impact on the probability of your success.

Some hunters use a piece of blaze orange material as they are trying to call a bird. The most common method is to sit below a piece of orange ribbon tied around a tree. This alerts other hunters to your presence, yet you run less risk of spooking a turkey than if you were wearing the blaze orange.

Various studies have shown that using blaze orange while trying to call a gobbler lowers hunter success by 30-60 percent. But some hunters believe the extra challenge is worth the extra margin of safety.

If you do use orange, use it correctly. Some shades of orange appear red under some low-light conditions and have actually *caused* turkey hunting accidents. Use a large piece of blaze orange, preferably tied around a tree.

Safe Hunting Techniques

In turkey hunting, there are certain techniques that can increase your safety; others that can set the stage for disaster. Here are some tips:

● Always call in terrain that is fairly open and allows you to see at least 50 yards in every direction. This lets you see any hunters that approach.

● Call from a position where you are protected from the back. Keeping your back against a rockpile, stump, or tree trunk wider than your shoulders and higher than your head will protect you if a negligent hunter sneaks up from behind and mistakes you for a turkey.

● If you see another hunter approaching, hold still and whistle or shout loudly. Try to get his attention while he is still out of shotgun range. Never wave, stand, or sound a turkey call. Any of these latter signals may be mistaken and cause him to fire.

● Never try to sneak in on a turkey for a shot, and generally avoid using a gobbler call when you know other hunters are in the area. These two tips are related: If you try to sneak up on a bird, it may turn out to be another caller. There is a chance either of you could mistake the other for a turkey. If you sound a gobbler call, the roles could be reversed; you could become the hunted.

Avoid sitting with your head visible over an obstruction. If you move, another hunter could mistake the round shape for the body of a wild turkey.

It's true that a gobbler call can be an asset in hunting, sometimes getting a tom turkey "fired up" when no other call works. But if you do use one, make sure you are in a safe calling position—in which you are protected from behind and can see any hunter approach from the front or sides.

• Never shoot at a sound or a movement. Assume every sound you hear and movement you see is another hunter. Never point your gun, take the safety off, or put your finger on the trigger until you have *positively* identified the target as a turkey and know that the background is safe for a shot.

Never try to sneak up on a turkey you hear; it could be another hunter calling. If you see another hunter approach, hold still and shout to get his attention while he is still at a safe distance.

• When walking in the woods in the dark, always use a flashlight. This not only identifies you as a person to other hunters, but helps you avoid injuries from a fall or other accident.

• Be aware of turkey fever and its prevention. Hunters have been known to hyperventilate in close encounters with turkeys. In the excitement of the hunt, it is easy to see what you are looking for, rather than what is there. Chances of this are increased if the hunter is inexperienced, fatigued, or has poor eyesight. For an ambitious hunter, it is tempting to take risks. The right attitude, with safety foremost, greatly reduces the odds of a mishap.

• Disregard peer pressure that places such urgent importance on getting a gobbler that it causes you to take chances.

• Remember that any time you use a turkey decoy, you are increasing the chance of an accident. If you must use a decoy, use it only in fairly open woods where you could see a hunter approach. Position the decoy and yourself so you are not in any possible line of fire if a hunter shoots at your decoy. This may be with a big tree behind you and with an open view or solid obstruction on the other side of the decoy. Position the decoy so it can be seen from the sides, not from in front or behind you. Use only hen turkey decoys, never a fake or mounted gobbler.

- Some situations may require you to run, such as to head off a moving gobbler or to break up a flock of turkeys. Be sure of your footing and control the muzzle of your gun.
- Be extremely careful to avoid inhaling and choking on a mouth diaphragm. Always take it from your mouth when you're not calling.
- Don't use a headnet that obscures your vision.

Photo by Mike Strandlund

After an immediately fatal shot, a turkey may flap its wings violently for several seconds. Get to the bird quickly, but be careful of being struck by wings and spurs.

• If you're on land where you have sole permission to hunt, don't assume that there are no other hunters around. That attitude may prompt you to take chancey shots.

• Be especially careful of the target's long-range background when using a rifle or handgun to shoot at a turkey.

• Get to a turkey as quickly as possible after shooting, but be careful if it is struggling—slashing spurs can cause severe cuts. Step on the head and pin down the body with your hands.

• Never crowd another hunter working a bird.

• When hunting with companions, be certain of each other's location.

• Avoid areas with high hunting pressure.

• Discuss safety techniques with companions.

• Remember that poachers and other blatantly irresponsible hunters may be nearby. Take every possible precaution—never assume that other hunters are reasonably safe.

Safety Afield

Many of the safety concerns a turkey hunter must remember have nothing to do with guns. They include the ever-present dangers of being in the woods: falls and similar mishaps; hypothermia; thirst and starvation.

Being careful and "staying found" will prevent most of these. Use common sense; keep safety in mind. Always carry maps and a compass if there is a possibility of getting lost (even in familiar country) and know how to use them. Make sure that someone knows where you are going and when you plan to be back. Carry a first-aid kit, maybe a snake-bite kit, and signalling devices.

Hypothermia, or severe loss of body heat, is a little-understood affliction. It is one of the biggest threats to the outdoorsman, possible in temperatures as warm as 60 degrees under certain conditions. Wet clothes, wind, and fatigue contribute to hypothermia.

Persons suffering from hypothermia go through stages beginning with shivering and progressing to loss of muscular control, mental confusion, and unconsciousness. Victims may have very pale skin, rigid muscles, and may be unable to speak.

To help prevent hypothermia, wear clothes that offer good protection in wind and wet, such as rain suits or nylon shell jackets, combined with wool or good synthetic insulation. Dress in layers. If you think there is a good chance of getting wet, you may be able to bring a change of dry clothes in a waterproof bag. Don't overexert yourself, as tiredness lowers resistance to cold. Take precautions from getting wet. Carry sources of heat,

The possibility of hypothermia, or exposure, is one of the most dangerous elements in hunting. The most common causes are dressing too lightly for the weather, becoming lost, and getting wet.

such as warm drinks in thermos bottles, firebuilding material, or camp stoves, etc.

Persons suffering from hypothermia often don't realize the seriousness of the situation. They should be warmed with blankets, warm water, hot drinks, or the body heat of companions.

The best prevention for hypothermia, as well as all problems afield, is planning and common sense.

Turkey Hunting Ethics

Safety is just one consideration in hunting ethics, which encompasses all the responsibilities a hunter has to other hunters, landowners, the general public, and the game. Governments require certain generally accepted ethical behavior through hunting laws and regulations. In other cases, the hunter himself has the obligation to decide what is right, what is wrong, and hunt according to those standards.

Some ethical questions are simple: Any responsible turkey hunter would abhor shooting a nesting hen. Others are more complex and open for debate: Is it acceptable to shoot a roosting gobbler? Should I try to call a turkey that another hunter is working? I heard a gobble just on the other side of that *No Trespassing* sign—should I go for it?

Most ethical questions can be resolved by answering the questions, is it legal or, is it fair to everyone concerned, including the game and myself? There are standards to follow, but ultimately, you must decide.

171

Photo by Charlie Farmer

Many persons hunt mainly for the peace of mind they find in the outdoors. Don't violate their rights by disturbing them or littering. Also, by showing respect for property, whether public or private, will improve your chances of being welcome again. Violations of property laws is the leading cause of land being posted off-limits to hunters.

Responsibility to Other Hunters

Besides safety, you have several other responsibilities to your fellow hunters. If you find another hunter working a gobbler you planned to hunt, bow out and look for another bird. Moving in on another hunter is not only discourteous and unfair, but also unsafe and counterproductive. Hopefully, another hunter will someday show you the same respect.

Try to pass on responsible hunting behavior to fellow hunters. If a new hunter seems to be going astray, try to educate him in hunting ethics. If a companion refuses to hunt responsibly, refuse to hunt with him.

Don't litter, drive vehicles where others may be hunting, or otherwise disturb other people or the area. Most hunters have deep feelings for nature and the peace of mind they find while hunting. Don't violate them.

Responsibilities to Landowners

One example of how hunters hurt themselves through poor ethics is the alienation of landowners. Each year, thousands of acres of private land are posted off limits because hunters treated the land or its owner with disrespect. It hurts all hunters.

Always get permission before hunting on any private property. Approach the landowner with courtesy—not only because you will have a better chance of getting permission, but to promote the image of the hunter. Once you receive permission, treat the land with the utmost care. Leave no signs you were there—take spent shells and litter with you, and maybe pick up some litter left by others. Don't drive on soft ground and leave tire ruts.

Other ways to keep good landowner relations are to avoid disturbing livestock, fences, crops, and other property. Don't abuse your welcome by bringing a carload of companions or hunting on the land day after day.

A token of appreciation such as a gift, a card, or offer to help with chores goes a long way toward being welcome next year.

Responsibilities to the Public

Remember that the environment and animals belong to everyone, not just hunters. Respect the rights of people who enjoy nature without hunting—avoid shooting in areas where you know nonhunters are enjoying the outdoors. Keep shell cases, gut piles, and other signs of hunting out of view. Don't display bagged animals to people who may not want to see them. Remember that unfavorable public opinion has resulted in laws and regulations of adverse impact to hunters.

Another duty the hunter owes the public is to ensure the enforcement of all laws. Hunters must abide by the laws and report those who trespass, poach animals, shoot road signs, or otherwise vandalize property.

Responsibility to the Game

The magnificent wild turkey, like all game animals, deserves the greatest respect and most humane treatment a hunter can give his prey. Hunters who do not feel a certain reverence for a turkey and an obligation to conserve the resource are missing the essence of hunting.

Never take a shot that has a strong chance of crippling a turkey. This includes shots at marginal range and at birds that have their vital areas protected but nonvital areas exposed.

Under no circumstances should you shoot indiscriminately into a flock. Always identify your target; be especially careful in the spring, when killing a hen probably also kills a dozen or so poults. If you take a shot at a gobbler, be certain there is no hen lurking in the background that could be killed by the shot. While spring hunting, pass up bearded hens even though they may be legal game. They may have a dozen eggs ready to hatch.

Photo by Ron Keil, Ohio Department of Natural Resources

Are they in range? Is that another turkey behind the gobbler on the left? Could you injure another turkey if you shoot at one? These are among the many questions a hunter must ask—and answer—before he presses the trigger.

Carefully consider whether you would shoot at a running or flying bird, and under which circumstances you would not. Make full use of the meat and trophy of a bagged bird.

Do your part in conservation and promotion of turkeys. In doing so, you are also conserving and promoting the future of turkey hunting. One way to get involved is to join the National Wild Turkey Federation, Inc., Wild Turkey Center, P.O. Box 530, Edgefield, SC 29824. The National Rifle Association (11250 Waples Mill Rd., Fairfax, VA 22030) conducts turkey hunting clinics, provides members with a hunter information service, and offers other benefits to hunters and gun owners.

Responsibilities to Yourself
Finally, don't forget your responsibilities to yourself. If a certain law or hunting regulation conflicts with your well-considered ethical beliefs, work to change that law. Fight it with letters and votes, not disobedience.

Don't take a chance or violate your ethics in a way that you may regret later. By the same token, hunt hard, hunt honestly, and be proud of your sportsmanship.

Pass Along the Tradition
If you're a hunter in the truest sense, you will eventually reach a point where you derive the most hunting satisfaction from introducing others to the sport. It may be acquainting a friend with hunting, taking a young boy or girl on their first hunt, or volunteering in a hunter education program.

Talk with the new hunter about hunting responsibilities and

ethics that all hunters should abide. Show respect for game by never taking a chancy shot, by making every effort to recover a wounded animal, and by never wasting bagged game. Make him or her realize why they must also treat landowners and the general public with respect, to prevent prejudice against hunters. Instruct new hunters early on safety, ethics, and responsibility because their respect and appreciation of our hunting heritage will determine the future of hunting.

Photo Courtesy Missouri Department of Conservation

With our increasingly cosmopolitan society, the future of hunting is uncertain. Protection of our sporting tradition lies with a new generation of knowledgeable, responsible hunters. Teach them well.

Appendix

THE NRA AND HUNTING

T he National Rifle Association of America encourages and supports sport hunting through a wide variety of programs and services.

The NRA Hunter Services Department assists state and provincial hunter education programs with support materials and training programs for professional and volunteer staff. NRA Hunter Clinics answer the demand for advanced education by emphasizing skills, responsibility; and safety as applied to hunting techniques and game species. The Hunter Services Department communicates to the members a variety of information necessary to plan and complete hunts. The NRA International Youth Hunter Education Challenge offers a series of events on the local, state, and national levels to challenge young hunters, through hunting-simulated events, to apply basic skills learned in the classroom. Financial support for wildlife management and shooting sports research is available through the NRA Environment Conservation & Hunting Outreach Program.

The NRA Institute for Legislative Action protects the legal rights of hunters. NRA publications provide a variety of printed material on firearms, equipment, and techniques for hunters, including *American Hunter* Magazine, the largest periodical in the U.S. devoted to hunting. Junior programs encourage young people to participate in hunting. Special insurance benefits are available to NRA hunting members, and hunters can further benefit by joining an NRA hunting club or by affiliating an existing club with the NRA. The NRA works with other hunting organizations to sustain a positive image of hunting as a traditional form of recreation, to combat anti-hunting efforts, and to promote a life-long interest in hunting.

For further information, contact the National Rifle Association of America, Hunter Services Department, 11250 Waples Mill Road, Fairfax, Va. 22030. Telephone (703) 267-1500.

NATIONAL RIFLE ASSOCIATION OF AMERICA

T he National Rifle Association (NRA), chartered in 1871, is not only the oldest shooting and hunting organization in America, it is also an educational, recreational and public service organization dedicated to the right of responsible citizens to own and use firearms for all legitimate purposes.

The NRA is a nonprofit organization supported entirely by its over 2.8 million members and 10,000 affiliated clubs. It is not affiliated with any arms or ammunition manufacturers. Although it receives no appropriations from the Congress, the NRA cooperates with all branches of the U.S. skilled forces, Federal agencies, States, and local governments interested in teaching firearms skills and safety to interested Americans.

The NRA's Hunter Services Department has several departmental programs that seek to expand the hunter's knowledge and skills and to foster the hunter's tradition of sharing the bounty of the hunt. The Wildlife Management Program promotes and defends hunting as a viable and necessary method of improving the propagation of and providing for the wise use of renewable wildlife resources. As an integral part of that program, the Environment, Conservation and Hunting Outreach (ECHO) Program is a grant program that the NRA has developed to provide financial and technical assistance to youth organizations such as the 4-H, Future Farmers of America and Boy Scouts of America, as well as to wildlife and land management agencies, research centers, hunting and shooting clubs and conservation organizations that undertake wildlife habitat improvement and hunting related projects in cooperation with the NRA. Such projects include habitat improvements, providing hunting opportunities for handicapped hunters, hunter access improvement, shooting range improvement, modification of shooting facilities to accommodate handicapped shooters, conservation education and hunter education.

The Youth Hunting Skills and Schools/National Tours and Clinics Program promotes hunter safety and education, defends hunting as a sound wildlife management practice and supports the long standing hunting heritage through the distribution of literature such as the Hunter Education Brochure series, the Hunter Skills series and the NRA Hunter's Guide. As primary components of this program, the Youth Hunter Education Challenge (YHEC) provides advanced hunter education to some 20,000 participants each year, and the Great American Hunters Tour (GAHT) provides educational seminars from nationally known hunting experts to over 30,000 attendees each year.

The Hunter Services Department operates the NRA's "Hunters for the Hungry Information Clearinghouse." The Clearinghouse helps to put NRA members in touch with local Hunters for the Hungry programs so these hunters can share their wild game harvests with those less fortunate in their community, as a high protein food source. The NRA assists in fund raising to help with food processing and distribution, and provides assistance to persons or organizations who wish to start a new program in their own area.

Well managed hunting is a beneficial use of renewable wildlife resources that when left to nature, are lost to predation, disease, starvation or old age. Proper hunting is in complete accord with the moral tenets and historical facts of human existence. The hunting heritage predates recorded history by many centuries. The hunter's participation in the chase today is a healthy exercise, both physically and spiritually.

The hunter's interest in wildlife has been the principal factor in fostering sound management and conservation practices. Provision for the hunter's harvest provides the incentive for the hunter's contribution, without which all else would be lost. The commitment of the hunter's contributions of voluntary taxing, licensing and regulation assure the propogation of all wildlife.

Hunting is dominant among American traditions and has contributed substantially to our strong national character. Its future is a primary concern of the NRA.

The following materials are available from the NRA Sales Department and can help you prepare for your next hunt.

To order any of the materials listed below, Telephone (800) 336-7402.

Description

NRA Hunter Skills Series
(Soft Cover)
Wild Turkey Hunting
Whitetail Deer Hunting
Waterfowl Hunting
Muzzleloader Hunting
Bowhunting
Upland Game Bird Hunting
Western Big Game Hunting

NRA Hunter Skill Series
(Hardbound Versions)
Whitetail Deer Hunting
Muzzleloader Hunting
Bowhunting
Upland Game Bird Hunting
Wild Game Cook Book

Brochures
Turkey Hunting Safety
Wild Game Field to Table
Firearm Safety and the Hunter
Landowner Relations
Responsible Hunting
Hypothermia
Fitness and Nutrition
Water Safety
Tree Stand Safety
Hunting's Future? It's Up To You
Hunting and Wildlife Management
Eye and Ear Care

Description

Life Size Game Targets

Sighting Duck
Black Bear
Coyote
Javelina
Mule Deer
Pheasant
Pronghorn
Red Fox
Whitetail Deer
Duck
Groundhog
Cottontail
Squirrel
Turkey

ORDERING INFORMATION

- Use the NRA Standard Order Form to order items listed, or call 1-800-336-7402.
- Prices are subject to change without notice.
- Prices do not include state taxes or handling, packing, and shipping charges.
- Order forms and current prices are available from the NRA Sales Department, P.O. Box 5000, Kearneysville, WV 25430-5000, or call (800)336-7402 between 9 a.m. and 9 p.m. Eastern time, Monday through Friday.

THE NRA HUNTER SKILLS SERIES

T he NRA Hunter Skills Series is a developing library of books on hunting, shooting, and related activities. It supports the NRA Hunter Clinic Program, a national network of seminars conducted by the NRA Hunter Services Division and volunteer hunter clinic instructors.

The hunter training manuals are developed by NRA staff, with the assistance of noted hunting experts, hunter educators, experienced outdoor writers, and representatives of hunting/conservation organizations. The publications are available in student (bound) and instructor (loose leaf) editions.

The program is planned to include clinics and support material on hunting whitetail deer, waterfowl, wild turkey, small game, predators, upland game, western big game, and others. It will also address marksmanship and hunting with rifle, shotgun, muzzleloader, handgun, and archery equipment.

For more information about the NRA Hunter Clinic Program and its training materials, contact the National Rifle Association of America, Hunter Services Department, 11250 Waples Mill Road, Fairfax, Va. 22030. Telephone (703) 267-1500.